APPROPRIATE BEHAVIOR

Queer Film Classics
Edited by Matthew Hays and Thomas Waugh

The enduring commercial success of LGBTQ2I films over recent generations offers proof of widespread interest in queer film within both pop culture and academia. Not only are recent works riding the wave of the new maturity of queer film culture, but a century of queer and proto-queer classics are in busy circulation thanks to a burgeoning online queer cinephile culture and have been brought back to life by omnipresent festivals and revivals. Meditations on individual films from queer perspectives are particularly urgent, unlocking new understandings of political as well as aesthetic and personal concerns.

Queer Film Classics at McGill-Queen's University Press emphasizes good writing, rigorous but accessible scholarship, and personal, reflective thinking about the significance of each film – writing that is true to the film, original, and enlightening and enjoyable for film buffs, scholars, and students alike. Books in the series are short – roughly 40,000 words – but well illustrated and allow for considerable depth. Exploring historical, authorial, and production contexts and drawing on filmic analysis, these open-ended essays also develop the author's personal interests or a subjective reading of the work's sexual identity discourses or reception. The series aims to meet the diversity, quality, and originality of classics in the queer film canon, broadly conceived, with equally compelling writing and critical insight. Books in the series have much to teach us, not only about the art of film but about the queer ways in which films can transmit our meanings, our stories, and our dreams.

L'Homme blessé
Robert Payne

Boys Don't Cry
Chase Joynt and Morgan M Page

Orlando
Russell Sheaffer

Appropriate Behavior
Maria San Filippo

APPROPRIATE BEHAVIOR

Maria San Filippo

McGill-Queen's University Press
Montreal & Kingston | London | Chicago

© McGill-Queen's University Press 2022

ISBN 978-0-2280-1457-7 (cloth)
ISBN 978-0-2280-1458-4 (paper)
ISBN 978-0-2280-1568-0 (ePDF)
ISBN 978-0-2280-1569-7 (ePUB)

Legal deposit fourth quarter 2022
Bibliothèque nationale du Québec

Printed in Canada on acid-free paper that is 100% ancient forest free (100% post-consumer recycled), processed chlorine free

Library and Archives Canada Cataloguing in Publication

Title: Appropriate behavior / Maria San Filippo.
Names: San Filippo, Maria, author.
Description: Series statement: Queer film classics | Includes bibliographical references and index.
Identifiers: Canadiana (print) 20220274312 | Canadiana (ebook) 20220274398 | ISBN 9780228014584 (softcover) | ISBN 9780228014577 (hardcover) | ISBN 9780228015680 (PDF) | ISBN 9780228015697 (ePUB)
Subjects: LCSH: Appropriate behavior. | LCSH: Akhavan, Desiree, 1984—Criticism and interpretation. | LCSH: Bisexuality in motion pictures.
Classification: LCC PN1997.2.A67 S26 2022 | DDC 791.43/72—dc23

This film is my ode to all the romantic encounters in my life.
Desiree Akhavan

This book is dedicated to all the loves of my life.
Maria San Filippo

Contents

Acknowledgments | ix
Synopsis | xi
Credits | xiii

Prelude: Queering the Classic | 3
Act I: "Superficial, Homophobic Lesbians" | 6
Act II: "A Gay *Annie Hall*" | 43
Act III: "An Iranian Bisexual Teacher" | 82
Finale: *The Bisexual* and Beyond | 110
Encore: "A Sociopath Who Keeps a Low Overhead": A Dialogue with Desiree Akhavan | 114
"Oh Shadow" by Juan Boscán Almogávar | 135

Notes | 137
References | 141
Index | 153

Acknowledgments

First and foremost, I wish to thank Jonathan Crago, Matthew Hays, and Thomas Waugh for granting me the opportunity to compose and send out into the world this love letter to *Appropriate Behavior*. I am honoured to have been welcomed into the Queer Film Classics clan, and deeply appreciative of the editorial expertise, collegiality, and encouragement that they and the anonymous reviewers provided.

This book's gestation spanned two of the most fraught years in modern global history; that I was able to devote energies to such a pleasurable pursuit during unprecedentedly trying times is credit to the generous professional support offered by my home institution, Emerson College.

I extend my thanks to Cecilia Frugiuele of Parkville Pictures for facilitating the reproduction of images from *Appropriate Behavior* – among her many formidable efforts as the film's producer. Thanks also to Louisa Maycock of Girls on Tops for granting permission to reproduce an image from the company's website.

Thank you to Dr Alix Ingber, professor emerita of Spanish at Sweet Briar College, for permitting me to reprint her beautiful translation of "Oh Sombra," and thank you as well to Susana Reisman for pointing the way.

Thanks to Hannah Plotka and Lids Bierenday for providing ace assistance with this manuscript's research, preparation, and promotion. My gratitude also goes out to the team at McGill-Queen's University Press for their labours on this book's behalf, and to Kathryn Simpson for their skilful copyediting.

I pay tribute to the journalists, critics, and scholars whose early appreciations of *Appropriate Behavior* were foundational for my own. I wish particularly to thank Claire Perkins and Michele Schreiber for including my ode to Desiree Akhavan and Ingrid Jungermann's work in their 2019 "Independent Women: From Film to Television" special issue of *Feminist Media Studies*, and to thank Clara Bradbury-Rance for our generative collaboration as co-chairs of the "Queer Re-significations" panel at the 2021 Society for Cinema and Media Studies Conference, where I presented my work on Akhavan's *The Bisexual*.

Thank you to Maya Montañez Smukler and Jennifer Moorman for sharing their expertise in crafting interview questions (even if I promptly went off-script once my discussion with Akhavan commenced).

My family, friends, and colleagues are an enduring source of support through all my endeavours, as I navigate making my work the best it can be without it being all of me.

From first viewing *Appropriate Behavior* to finishing my final edit, I was grateful and privileged to have had Vernon Shetley by my side and (as always) as my best editor; this book and I are stronger for it, and our mutual appreciation for this film is preserved in these pages.

Finally, and most of all, I thank Desiree Akhavan for her work.

Synopsis

Brooklyn, circa 2013. Twentysomething Shirin, teary-eyed, rides the New York City subway en route to pick up her belongings following her break-up with Maxine, who speaks only to insist she take back the dildo and strap-on harness that had been Shirin's gift. Attempting to dispose of them in a dumpster only to retrieve them seconds later, Shirin walks dejectedly away, sex toy in hand, as the credits appear onscreen. Meeting up with pal Crystal, Shirin mopingly recalls her lacklustre-of-late sex life with Maxine but cannot be stopped from trying (and failing) to charm her way back on to Maxine's shift at the Park Slope Coop. Visiting her Iranian parents Nasrin and Mehrdad along with brother Ali and his fiancée Layli, both successful surgeons, Shirin neglects to mention the breakup and evades their questions about her love life. Meanwhile, having been recommended by Crystal to absent-minded stoner Ken for a job teaching filmmaking, Shirin is dismayed to find herself caring for a rowdy brood of boys "roughly a decade younger" than she'd been expecting and is further demoralized upon meeting the supercilious Tibet, who teaches the (all-girls) advanced class next door. Again Shirin evades full disclosure when her family helps her move into the dilapidated Brooklyn loft occupied by stone-faced goth couple Felicia and Jacques, and is reminded when unpacking *Stone Butch Blues* of Maxine buying it "to educate" her. Later Shirin conjures up wistfully the New Year's Eve party where she and Maxine first met and kissed, then the Nowruz celebration Maxine attended closeted as Shirin's "white friend." After sex with a hot dim guy she meets online, Shirin falls into another reverie of first exchanging "I love yous" with Maxine, though on her next flashback they're paid a visit by Shirin's parents, whose curiosity about the one bed in their apartment Shirin explains by fibbing, to Maxine's evident dislike. Back in the present, Shirin's subsequent attempt to make Maxine jealous by asking out foxy lawyer Sasha ends awkwardly, as does her ensuing threesome with swinger couple Marie and Ted. Walking home, she passes the bar where she fought with Maxine after catching her drunkenly kissing a guy on Pride. Attempting some retail therapy, Shirin is prodded into buying pricey lingerie by a haughty proprietress as a disbelieving Crystal looks on, prompting a recollection of the break-up fight where Maxine cut up her underwear. When they see each other at a club thereafter, Shirin, accompanied by hipster John Francis, makes a scene upon learning Maxine is dating Tibet and storms off to the bathroom, where Maxine eventually finds and assures her kindly but firmly that she'll be okay. Having conceived and created a movie "about farts," Shirin's class premieres their film alongside that of the advanced class; afterward, Ken congratulates Shirin and manages for the first time to address her correctly. Back at Nowruz one year later, Shirin manages to come out to her brother and, after stumbling and singeing a scarf during the fire ritual, attempts the same with her mother, who shushes her. Reporting it to Crystal as they travel by subway, she vows to try again then, at the next stop, catches sight of Maxine on the platform. They exchange a tentative wave, the train leaves the station, and after an extended hold on Shirin's face the screen goes black.

Credits

Appropriate Behavior (alternate title: *Appropriate Behaviour*), 2014, US, English, 86 minutes, colour, sound, RED Scarlet, 1.85:1
Filmed in Brooklyn, New York, US
MPAA rating: Not rated
Production company: Parkville Pictures

Director-screenwriter: Desiree Akhavan
Producer: Cecilia Frugiuele
Executive producers: Oliver Kaempfer, Hugo Kaempfer, Lucas Kaempfer, Katie Mustard
Director of photography: Chris Teague
Production designer: Miren Marañón
Editor: Sara Shaw
Casting director: Allison Twardziak
Music: Josephine Wiggs
Costume designer: Sarah Maiorino
Set designer: Amy E. Bishop
Special thanks: Ira Sachs

Principal cast
Desiree Akhavan   Shirin

Rebecca Henderson	Maxine
Halley Feiffer	Crystal
Scott Adsit	Ken
Arian Moayed	Ali
Anh Duong	Nasrin
Hooman Majd	Mehrdad
Aimee Mullins	Sasha
Chris Baker	Ted
Robyn Rikoon	Marie
Rosalie Lowe	Tibet
Kelly McAndrew	Lingerie Saleswoman
Justine Cotsonas	Layli
James C. Bristow	Henry (BrooklynBoy82)
Annalisa Graziano	Felicia
Michael Lonergan	Jacques
Cody DeFranco	John Francis
uncredited	Carrington

World premiere: 18 January 2014 (Sundance Film Festival)
Distributors: Gravitas Ventures (US), Peccadillo Pictures (UK)
DVD release: Kino Lorber (US)

APPROPRIATE BEHAVIOR

Prelude
Queering the Classic

As its title announces with equal measures of aspiration and irony, *Appropriate Behavior* both seeks approval and dryly defies any such mandate – be it artistic or societal – towards conformity or compliance. In proposing Desiree Akhavan's 2014 debut feature film for the Queer Film Classics series, I exert my own prerogative to "have it both ways" – to reappropriate a common charge made against us bisexuals – by arguing the case for *Appropriate Behavior* as a queer film classic, while simultaneously proposing that it "queers" the very concept of a classic.

To start, this volume is the series' first entry – rather belated, I'd say – on a film created by and centred on a bisexual woman (and a bisexual woman of colour at that). As someone with a personal and professional investment in sounding the often-silent letter in the middle of LGBTQ and in spotlighting women filmmakers, I bring to this project an unabashed interest in staking out space in the canon for a film I find both iconic and idiosyncratic. As much as Akhavan herself perceives *Appropriate Behavior*, as expressed in the 2020 interview that concludes this volume, to be "a love story, first and foremost," that classical premise belies her radical refashioning. Queer cinema is held to an overly exacting expectation that it tell "universal stories" that (straight) viewers will find "relatable," whereas – as act I indicates – *Appropriate Behavior*'s ambition lies beyond mainstream appeal. At the same time, *Appropriate*

Behavior stands apart from the gay coming out stories and lesbian period dramas that populate the contemporary LGBTQ+ film marketplace. With its distinctive voice and irreverent sensibility, *Appropriate Behavior* holds its own in a series boasting book-length odes to transgressors like *Arabian Nights*, *Boys in the Sand*, *Female Trouble*, *Scorpio Rising*, and *Trash*, even as it breaches what has long been a (gay) boys' club.

Appropriate Behavior appears additionally conspicuous among its Queer Film Classics cohort as its youngest and briefest entry, released in 2014 and lasting a mere 86 minutes. A further count against its claims to canonical status is its being a romantic comedy – that most critically maligned of film genres apart, perhaps, from pornography. Moreover, it was made by a twenty-nine-year-old first-time filmmaker who confesses she now finds it cringe-inducing, citing particularly its heaping of scatological humour; "It's like forty per cent fart jokes," she protested to *Fresh Air* host Terry Gross during their 2018 interview (Akhavan and Danforth), and again to me in our conversation transcribed at book's end. Even if Akhavan remains unrepentant about having a narrative structure stolen from *Annie Hall* (1977), that hallowed film's heteronormativity too would seem an inapt formula for achieving canonicity as a *queer* classic.

In still another sense, as we'll see, *Appropriate Behavior* demands a reconceptualization of "film classic" for being inextricably linked to Akhavan's earlier and later works of semi-autobiographical self-skewering: the co-created web series *The Slope* (2010–12) and the six-episode television series *The Bisexual* (2018). While this book's focus is on *Appropriate Behavior*, it bears noting, at the outset, the film's central position within an intertwined trilogy that cumulatively narrates Akhavan's "growing sideways" – queer scholar Kathryn Bond Stockton's 2009 coinage in characterizing the non-linear and anti-teleological path taken by queer subjects in a straight world. *Appropriate Behavior* constitutes, then, one-third of a tripartite *Künstlerroman* portraying Akhavan's self-becoming as a media creator; as such, it develops further this book series' queer conception of the *film* canon through its platform-crossing non-singularity as a web-, film-, and television-spanning trilogy – albeit one that additionally expands and complicates our concept of the trilogy form (see Perkins and Verevis 2021, 1–31).

Far from seeking to impose a version of the exclusionary gravitas that traditional canons enforce, this book aims instead to, as film scholar Rebecca Harrison's 2018 #MeToo manifesto put it, "fuck the canon." It's an aim inherent to the Queer Film Classics series, as evidenced by the parallel history of cinema it constructs. Yet as Harrison's choice of wording reveals, there's a lingering desire for domination (or perhaps submission) where the canon is concerned, that works not to destroy the canon but to redeploy, or reappropriate, its power. However vulgar, the "class" that canonicity confers in anointing a film "a classic" must be acknowledged, now especially, as independent and marginalized creators struggle to get their work made, seen, and remembered. To harness that power toward ends that are queer, feminist, and anti-racist is the vital task at which we (those of us so invested) toil. Hard as it is, this book – like the film it celebrates – is a labour of love.

Act I

"Superficial, Homophobic Lesbians"

I don't use language appropriately. I am always using the wrong words ... "Dyke" is one of those words. I use it with love, and I think it's a great word. I love the way it rolls off the tongue. Have I earned the right to use it as a bisexual woman? In the eyes of some people, no ... Right now I'm editing something, and one of the characters uses the word "fag." A lesbian uses the word. And I had a real discussion today about, you know, what are we going to think about that woman who uses that word? And is that appropriate? And this is the stuff that my life is built around. I'm really fascinated by the language people use and who's able to say what word.

Desiree Akhavan on *Fresh Air*

Instant Classic

The first question a reader of this volume may have is why a film released as recently as 2014 deserves recognition as a "Queer Film Classic," no matter how queerly conceived. Answering that question gives me the immensely pleasurable task of tallying the reasons why a work that might seem too recent and in other ways too ... inappropriate to achieve canonical status is so deserving. That I'm hardly alone in celebrating *Appropriate Behavior* and its defiantly bisexual, Iranian American creator Desiree Akhavan also makes my task easier. That the film was widely acclaimed upon release, and since, does not mean, however, that Akhavan's triumph was accomplished easily or overnight. Taking a cue from *Appropriate Behavior*'s nonlinear exposition, I begin by retracing the circuitous path that Akhavan's debut feature took to becoming a queer film classic.

Seeking to capitalize on the success of her attention-getting web series *The Slope* (2010–12) Akhavan's first attempts to source funding from cultural nonprofits fell flat; as she observed, "I just don't think I fit the mould of what you want for your Persian grant, or your women's grant or your gay grant." (Alcamo 2014). This outcome suggests that Akhavan's brand of work somehow falls in between the various identity categories around which nonprofit funding is organized. *Appropriate Behavior* would eventually be financed through private equity, which has become an increasingly essential resource for first-time filmmakers as the specialty divisions and independent distributors that had previously sustained indie filmmaking have disappeared. Once completed, *Appropriate Behavior* still needed to distinguish itself among the glut of indie films pouring into festival submission portals and streaming sites. Despite what one might judge its evident attractions to film festival programmers – an edgy comedy made by and starring a queer woman of colour and featuring sex, romance, and Brooklyn hipsters – Akhavan recalls having been rejected from thirty festivals with *Appropriate Behavior* (Wickham 2015). No wonder that the day she got the call from Sundance, after submitting a rough cut, seemed nothing short of miraculous. As she related, giddy with anticipation en route to Park City in January 2014, and calling upon an analogy that kids of the 1980s and '90s will appreciate: "I don't even know how to describe it, because never in my life have I had a dream that came true. It was the equivalent to me of like … I'm trying to think of who I had a crush on in sixth grade. It would be like Jonathan Taylor Thomas giving you a phone call and being like 'Hey babe, let's do this, wanna be my girlfriend?'" (Ehrlich 2015). Programmed in Sundance's NEXT section devoted to "pure, bold works distinguished by an innovative, forward-thinking approach to storytelling," *Appropriate Behavior*'s world premiere garnered an audience award nomination and positive notices in the trades and festival reportage. "Remember the name Desiree Akhavan. You're going to be hearing it a lot in the future." So began the *Washington Post*'s review of *Appropriate Behavior* (Merry 2015). "Akhavan's remarkable, near-perfect debut has wit and charisma to spare," wrote Inkoo Kang (2015) in *The Wrap*.

Following its Sundance triumph, *Appropriate Behavior* received a Grand Jury Prize at the San Diego Asian Film Festival, a Tangerine Entertainment Juice Award (for emergent women feature filmmakers) at the Provincetown International Film Festival, and the award for Screenwriting in a US Dramatic Feature at Outfest Los Angeles, alongside several additional nominations for jury prizes and audience awards at festivals as far-flung and multi-faceted as the Glasgow Film Festival, the Off-Camera International Festival of Independent Cinema in Poland, and Queer Lisboa in Portugal. The film's success at both identity-branded festivals and those programming a broader range of independent releases reflects Akhavan's success at creating a work that engages LGBTQ+ as well as BIPOC audiences while also being capable of crossing over to a wider audience. Commissioned to write a piece for the Gotham Film and Media Institute's (formerly IFP) website while in pre-production on *Appropriate Behavior*, Akhavan (2013) worried that her film would "end up premiering at the Hoboken Film Festival for Ambiguously Ethnic Women & The Gluten Intolerant and then be banished to the Gay & Lesbian section of Netflix." Though her concerns proved unfounded, Akhavan's snark here signals the solipsistic tendencies encouraged by the then-thriving if still circumscribed ecosystem of LGBTQ+-focused festivals and VOD sites like Buskfilms and QueerFrame.[1]

Staying aloft after a festival run has become increasingly challenging, given how few festival premieres result in theatrical distribution deals, even in an era when a limited release was still a reasonable aim for first-time filmmakers – though Akhavan found a different set of criteria applied to catapult her past the velvet rope that restricts indies clambering for theatrical exhibition. "On the indie film circuit and in the film festival world, it's very attractive to be a gay, Iranian film," observed Akhavan, "but then in the theatrical setting to get a distributor and a release, it's not" (Alcamo 2014). What propelled the film forward was the accumulating buzz of festival accolades, critical praise, and word-of-mouth, sufficiently voluble by summer of 2014 to entice the indie distributor Gravitas Ventures to venture a US limited theatrical release, with a "day and date" deal for simultaneous online availability in January 2015 – just shy of a year after its Sundance debut. It was subsequently picked up for UK distribution by queer film specialist Peccadillo Pictures, and given a wide release there the following March. Though box office returns were modest, award nominations established the film as a succès d'estime: for "Best First Screenplay" at the Independent Spirit Awards (the indie Oscars, as it's known) as well as for "Outstanding Film – Limited Release" at the GLAAD Media Awards, and Akhavan for "Bingham Ray Breakthrough Director" at the Gotham Awards. With these latter two commendations – the former doled out by the LGBTQ+ media watchdog not always known for finding the humour in the inappropriate (Akhavan's signature), the latter named for the daring indie distributor of films like *Drugstore Cowboy* (1989) and *Lost Highway* (1997) – both film and filmmaker demonstrated an aptitude for, if I may reappropriate the expression, "going both ways."

Having hovered in the high ninetieth percentile since its debut, at the time of this writing in 2021 *Appropriate Behavior* has a 95 per cent "Certified Fresh" rating on the Rotten Tomatoes critics' metre. The film's fandom cuts across categories of cultural identity, industry demographics, and taste preference to encompass, on one hand, cinephiles and (as Akhavan herself noted halfway through the film's festival run) "30–45-year-old straight men" (Alcamo 2014), and on the other, queer folx and Millennials/Gen Z'ers. *Appropriate Behavior*'s broad appeal surely derives from its singular blend of being "audacious, funny and unique" – so anointed in the promotional endorsement provided by Lena Dunham, to whom Akhavan would immediately and repeatedly be compared.

To make an attention-grabbing independent first feature – in entertainment industry lingo, a "calling card" – in 2014 was a daunting prospect. Even as the much-ballyhooed digital revolution enabled ever more films to be made, the 2008 economic downturn and an emerging shift to streaming was shuttering those studio specialty divisions and boutique distributors that had previously enabled modestly budgeted, low-concept films to find audiences. By 2014, indie filmmaker-turned-industry sage Mark Duplass was likening the resulting free-for-all to Reaganomics: an ecosystem driven by low-cost technology and labour and deregulated distribution channels, but unmatched by the requisite number of consumers needed to offset saturation or a profit incentive for financiers to back mid-range films, thus creating an increasingly bifurcated structure of economic disparity between blockbusters and no-budgets (Duplass 2014). In a 2014 *Salon* piece titled "America's Next Wal-Mart: The Indie Film Industry," entertainment industry reporter Beanie Barnes extended the Reaganomics metaphor, describing "an industry where steadily shrinking profits are privatized while growing costs/losses are increasingly socialized" (Barnes 2014). Like Duplass, Barnes was an early predictor of what has now come to pass: an oligopolistic structure wherein a few "big box" content providers control access to and reap most of the profit from the plethora of films and shows whose creators take on increasing amounts of risk and debt for decreasing possibilities of payoff.

Less than a year after *Appropriate Behavior*'s premiere, Duplass used his keynote address at the 2015 South by Southwest Film Festival to put a positive spin on the transition then underway: "As the death of the middle class of film has happened, it has been rebirthed in television. The way you used to make really awesome $5 million movies that didn't have movie stars in them and had really great, cool original content, that's happening in cable TV right now" (Bakare 2015). By the following summer, the proliferation of television channels developing original content led FX Networks chairman John Langraf, addressing the Television Critics Association on their summer press tour, to his famous proclamation of the industry having reached a quantity *and* quality highpoint: "Peak TV." As it turns out, the summit was still a ways off, as the number of scripted series continued to climb into 2020; only the COVID-19 pandemic put the (perhaps temporary) brakes on the proliferation of content.

Against these odds, and shouldering grad school debt and New York City rent, Akhavan stuck to the feature film route when so much start-up funding was being siphoned off into series television, then found a foothold on a path overcrowded with aspiring auteurs awakening to the reality that, as Duplass warned at the start of his SXSW keynote, "The cavalry isn't coming." Committing to feature filmmaking without significant financial backing mandated a microbudget (well below the $5 million "middle class" marker), a cast devoid of marquee talent, and when it came time to mount a publicity campaign, a premise provocative enough to cut through the clutter; *Appropriate Behavior* had all three. Modestly budgeted, the film was shot on location in Brooklyn featuring an eclectic ensemble, corralled by casting director Allison Twardziak, of recognizable (but far from household name) New York–based actors – and some non-actors – who deliver pitch-perfect performances. Yet the irrepressible frontwoman was the "triple threat" writer-director-actor Akhavan, who had already learned the value of provocative self-branding.

"Having It Both Ways"

From the 2010 short *Nose Job* that she made as her NYU graduate thesis film, to her self-billing as one-half of *The Slope*'s "superficial, homophobic lesbian" duo, to her television series *The Bisexual*, Akhavan has made it her mission to lean in to the cultural clichés applied to her and her alter egos, trading on their controversial currency. *Appropriate Behavior*'s logline cannily aligned itself with precisely the cultural identity markers that its underachieving protagonist, played by Akhavan, goes on to implode: "Shirin is struggling to become an ideal Persian daughter, politically correct bisexual and hip young

Figure 1
Desiree Akhavan on the set of *Appropriate Behavior*, directing the (uncredited) young performer who plays Carrington, stone-faced son of hapless stoner dad Ken (Scott Adsit).

Brooklynite but fails miserably in her attempt at all identities. Being without a cliché to hold onto can be a lonely experience." By situating her alter ego Shirin as decidedly anti-aspirational – unideal, un-PC, un-hip – Akhavan conjured the indie film version of "high-concept" (industry-speak for an easily communicable premise) to signal her beguiling blend of emotional rawness and arch irreverence. That combination was visually realized in the UK release's promotional one-sheet picturing Shirin dejectedly slumped on a grimy-cool club toilet, with hot pink lettering announcing the ironic title and auteur tag "Appropriate Behaviour: A Film by Desiree Akhavan." Meanwhile, across the Atlantic, the image chosen for both the one-sheet for the film's North

"Superficial, Homophobic Lesbians" 13

Figure 2
The image used on *Appropriate Behavior*'s anything-but promotional one-sheet, with accompanying blurb by *Girls* creator Lena Dunham.

American release and its subsequent DVD release by Kino Lorber is that which graces this book's cover. It shows Akhavan as Shirin in a moment of self-reflection that only upon closer inspection reveals her face to be framed by those of an embracing couple: the ones we'll come to know as the swingers with whom she has a semi-disastrous threesome.

These publicity materials permitted Akhavan to have her cake and eat it too. They show the film's "relatable" protagonist falling woefully short of any self-actualizing script, bound for self-exile in a grimy (if glam) bathroom, or the third wheel at the threesome … The logline reinforces her "lonely" outsiderdom even while linking her to the aspirational in-groups (Persian … bisexual … hip young Brooklynite) that potentially confer indie credibility and define her persona. Akhavan thus carved out multiple promotional pathways for (what she called) "a gay, Iranian film" while at the same time warning of

Appropriate Behavior's only gay-adjacent and (in Shirin's description) "half-assed Iranian" failure to conform to conventional identity categories. The promotional rollout thereby announced an unruly new woman in town; while its creator-star's BIPOC and B-word signifying promises a "for us, by us" level of authenticity, it candidly reveals her as ill-fitting to serve as role model for any identity group.

To successfully straddle industry, demographic, and cultural niches as *Appropriate Behavior* did, playing to critical tastemakers and audience sensibilities with equal success, demands considerable shape-shifting. This is not to allege that Akhavan's auteur persona-in-progress or *Appropriate Behavior*'s publicity campaign was mercenary; on the contrary, in staking her claim for auteur status and indie credibility on a blatant blurring of her autobiographical and fictionalized selves, Akhavan was instinctively continuing her unapologetic self-presentation begun in *The Slope*. In an interview given around the time of the Sundance screening, Akhavan links the film's title to Shirin's struggle to accept that "there are certain guidelines to fitting into any of the communities that she was born into … but just because of her nature she's always going to feel inappropriate" (Ehrlich 2014). This inability to fit in constitutes a key element of identity for both *Appropriate Behavior* and Akhavan herself.

An early academic treatment of *Appropriate Behavior* by Claire Perkins (2016, 148–50) points to the way that Akhavan's "in-between sensibility manifests as a commentary on the difficulty – and undesirability – of 'achieving' the social and temporal expectations of a range of intersecting identities." Perkins's invocation here of the term in-betweener (perhaps unintentionally) aligns with its usage in queer culture to signify a position or movement between binary identity formations that disrupts and resists those formations. *Tweener* (its shortened form) designates someone whose sexuality and/or gender identity is nonbinary – neither gay nor straight, neither masculine/butch nor feminine/femme. To be an in-betweener, then, is to embody a perspective of (non)belonging – a simultaneous inhabiting of insider and outsider positions in relation to a designated group, be it one composed around an identity formation, political coalition, or professional ecosystem.

In-betweener, then, as a description of Akhavan's positioning in the entertainment industry, refers to her working across media platforms (web series, film, television) and transnationally (born and raised a New Yorker, she relocated to London for a time in the mid-2010s). In-betweener refers further to Akhavan's straddling of indie and LGBTQ+ festival and distribution circuits, as she has continued to find homes for her work at both Sundance and NewFest, to be recognized with both Independent Spirit and GLAAD Media Award nominations, to get coverage in both *Filmmaker* and the *Advocate*. Still another vector of in-betweenness stems from Akhavan's racial, national, and ethnic identities – she identifies as a woman of colour, as a first-generation Iranian American, and as Persian.[2] Above all, in-betweenness is bisexuality's *sine qua non*; Akhavan's steadfast if admittedly ambivalent insistence on identifying as bisexual, in the face of resistance from both her biological family and her chosen queer cohort, finds poignant expression through *Appropriate Behavior*'s Shirin. Perhaps, then, Akhavan's commitment to the in-between was less a bug than a feature that helped propel her to the forefront of debut indie filmmakers circa 2014. Perhaps, too, *Appropriate Behavior* was able to stand out insofar as twenty-first-century US queer cinema was suffering from a noticeable deficiency of, well, queerness ...

"No Homo"

As defined by one of its seminal theorists, David M. Halperin: "Queer is by definition *whatever* is at odds with the normal, the legitimate, the dominant" (1997, 62). Halperin insists that queerness challenges not only *heteronormativity* (the perception of heterosexuality as the norm) but *homonormativity*: the assimilation of LGBTQ+ lives and expectations to heterosexual patterns and structures. In 2002, American cultural historian Lisa Duggan referred to "the new homonormativity" of LGBTQ+ politics as one "that does not contest dominant heteronormative assumptions and institutions, but upholds and sustains them, while promising the possibility of a demobilized gay constituency and a privatized, depoliticized gay culture anchored in domesticity and consumption" (2002, 179). Queer scholars like Duggan deplored this retreat into the private sphere, aligning it with the neoliberal surrender to individualism and the market, a surrender that found its fullest expression in the cause of marriage equality.

Reflecting this context, early twenty-first-century US indie cinema typically soft-pedalled queer representation to achieve mainstream palatability. So-called "crossover films" – those featuring central queer characters and storylines that found favour with broader segments of the viewing audience – rendered their advocacy for the civil rights of same-sex couples palatable by painting queer characters as politically docile and desexualized. Given their focus on couple formation, romantic comedies were particularly potent vehicles for such ideological work. Examining such films featuring same-sex relationships to ask, as Debra A. Moddelmog did in her 2009 article "Can Romantic Comedy Be Gay?," yielded a resounding "kind of," insofar as 1990s–00s gay romcoms – whose couples are near-uniformly white, affluent, and sexually chaste – were nonetheless denied the cultural approval doled out to romcom's straight couples in the requisite Public Affirmation scene so frequently placed at a film's denouement that it had by then acquired awareness as a romcom trope (2009, 162–73).

Unsurprisingly, the resulting works did not always find favour within LGBTQ+ community circles; Lisa Cholodenko's crossover hit *The Kids Are All Right* (2010), for instance, drew complaints and even ire for its allegedly retrograde tropes and assimilationist values (Halberstam 2010; Danuta Walters 2012, 917–33). Despite bearing the imprimatur of a lesbian director (though co-written with, as was often pointed out, a straight male screenwriter known for penning conventional romcoms), Cholodenko's autobiographically inspired feature read to queer critics as a dilution of her edgier 1997 debut *High*

Art, a Rainer Werner Fassbinder–styled tragic love triangle set in what was then lower Manhattan's heroin-chic art scene and starring Ally Sheedy (in an award-winning comeback role) and a not-yet-famous Patricia Clarkson as addicts and codependent lovers; one of its foremost provocations was in aligning lesbianism with drug addiction. Tellingly, it is the film Akhavan (2015a) cited, in an interview with the British Film Institute around the time of *Appropriate Behavior*'s release, as her favourite work of queer cinema, about which she recalls, "That film undid me a little … It satisfied the cinephile in me and the homo." *High Art* is, as well, the film that critic B. Ruby Rich singled out for having "defied all prior taboos of contemporary lesbian cinema by showing the dark side of lesbian society and having the nerve to go for an unhappy ending" (2013, 133). While tonally *Appropriate Behavior* aims for deadpan irony rather than *High Art*'s Fassbinderian high camp, their simpatico sensibilities are evidenced in their shared aesthetic of lushly photographed yet grittily depicted New York – 1990s SoHo/Tribeca for Cholodenko, 2010s Brooklyn for Akhavan – and in their intoxicating if knowing glimpses into their art world and hipster subcultures, as well as in their self-styled protagonists whose professional angling and sexual adventuring put them at odds with propriety.[3] So enamored of the film was Akhavan, she reports having betrayed her own mandate to cast Persian actors in the roles of Shirin's family members by selecting Spanish-Vietnamese performer Anh Duong to play Shirin's mother Nasrin, in homage to her role as *High Art*'s haughty boss Dominique (Alcamo 2014). Rather than join the ranks of feel-good LGBTQ+ romcoms pushing the gay marriage agenda, *Appropriate Behavior* fashioned itself after the imaginatively crafted, autobiographically inspired first films by women filmmakers – several of whom identified as lesbian, bi, or queer – who emerged in the 1990s indie boom, which alongside *High Art* gave us such quirky gems as *All Over Me* (1997), *But I'm a Cheerleader* (1999), *Go Fish* (1996), *Party Girl* (1995), and *Walking and Talking* (1997).[4]

If *The Slope* emerged out of Akhavan and co-creator Ingrid Jungermann's impulse to lampoon themselves and the queer Brooklynite subcultural milieu

Figures 3–4
Paying homage to New Queer Cinema: Anh Duong as Dominique in Lisa Cholodenko's *High Art* (1997) and as Shirin's mother Nasrin in *Appropriate Behavior*.

they inhabited, Akhavan recalls *Appropriate Behavior* as having been inspired by the then girlfriends "having a discussion about how we hated all gay films" (Akhavan and Danforth 2018). Even taking into account her evident hyperbole, US queer cinema seemed at that point to have run aground. Apart from the occasional flash of wit – John Cameron Mitchell's delightfully demented *Hedwig and the Angry Inch* (2001), Angela Robinson's lesbian spy spoof D.E.B.S. (2004), the zany misfire *I Love You Phillip Morris* (2009) – "queer" and "irony" were far from constant companions in the millennium's first decade. Like those outliers, *Appropriate Behavior* defines itself not (as in earlier eras) in opposition to the presumed straightness of mainstream cinema, but rather against LGBTQ+ narratives that lacked the edge – or more specifically, the irony – that characterizes queer cultural practice. To illustrate this distinction, allow me to borrow an (itself borrowed) utterance of Akhavan's (as Shirin) from *Appropriate Behavior*, parsed meaningfully between her and Maxine just on the cusp of exchanging their first "I love you."

> SHIRIN: That is so beautiful, no homo.
> MAXINE: What do you mean, "No homo?"
> SHIRIN: Oh, you don't know what no homo is? Okay. So "no homo" is this thing that rappers say to each other to, like, nullify the gayness of their words. They could be, like, "Those are some really fly jeans, man. No homo." Or, "Your song touched me. No homo."
> MAXINE: Like, "I like the way your dick tastes in my mouth. No homo."
> SHIRIN: [*chuckles*] Exactly … I feel really lucky to have met you.
> MAXINE: No homo?
> SHIRIN: Homo.

This dialogue's disregard for the rules of discourse established by politically correct queer culture, for which even reappropriated slurs like "homo" are typically anathema – especially when originating (as in this case) outside of queer circles – is exhibit A for Akhavan's linguistic irreverence, as admitted on *Fresh Air* in the quotation that begins act I, the spark of her artistic sensibility since *The Slope*. Following from David M. Halperin's definition of "queer" as that which opposes both homonormative and heteronormative, Maxine's appropriation of "no homo" displays her queer knowingness about hip hop culture and the exaggerated performance of heteromasculinity it models. In another defiant bit of "fence-straddling" Akhavan shows her appreciation for what queer and straight cultures have to teach one another, wittily expressed through recourse to two strategies that LGBTQ+ cinema of the aughts had lost amidst its "for us, by us" solipsism and Obama-era earnestness: translation and irony.

We'll return to discuss the former's importance when examining *Appropriate Behavior*'s care to speak across the aisle, to define its queer idiom for its not in-the-know audience – while the latter, I am suggesting, is a key marker of Akhavan's self-distancing from the sentimentally well-meaning or banal (or both) coming-out dramas and same-sex romances that had buffed the rough edges from what B. Ruby Rich had hailed in its 1990s heyday as New Queer Cinema (1992, 41–4). Rich coined this term in 1992 (the year that *Philadelphia* won over audiences and Oscar voters) to designate aesthetically daring, queer-themed works that refused to water down queer representation and queer politics to court straight audiences. By 2000, however, in an article titled "A Queer and Present Danger: The Death of New Queer Cinema?," Rich (questioningly) eulogized the passing of the moment, concluding that "the sheer volume diluted the content" (2013, 130).

A decade later, upon release of Cholodenko's *The Kids Are All Right* in 2010, the tendency for US-produced queer indies to steer safely away from provocation was reinforced further by the belt-tightening brought on first by the Great Recession, then by a growing need for easily categorizable on-demand digital content. The migration of queer content into the new golden age of US serial television left a void in LGBTQ+ feature filmmaking that was punctured only by soulful passion projects willed into existence, such as Dee Rees's debut *Pariah* (2011) and Barry Jenkins's Oscar-winning *Moonlight*

(2016) – sombre stories by and about marginalized individuals that nevertheless broke out, but were decidedly not comedies. In advance of making *Appropriate Behavior*, Akhavan found a platform for her distinctive brand of deadpan on a still smaller screen than television's, in the then-nascent realm of the web series …

"Fuck[ing] with the Medium"

Along with Cholodenko, the woman director that Akhavan most frequently names as an influence is the self-proclaimed "pariah of French cinema" (Secher 2015), Catherine Breillat, particularly her 2001 film *À ma soeur* (retitled *Fat Girl* for its US release), a film so meaningful to Akhavan that a frame capture showing its ungainly adolescent protagonist serves as the banner image on her Twitter profile. As Akhavan recalls, "When I saw [Breillat's *Fat Girl*], it was such an incredible moment of thinking: This is what filmmaking is, this is how you fuck with the medium. I see the way that sex is depicted in films as a feminist pursuit of mine … and that's something Breillat has done in all her work" (Mayer 2015, 147). While Breillat herself is a troubling figure for feminism, both her unflinching regard for what I term elsewhere the "corporealities" of bodies and her frank appraisal of the gendered power dynamics pervading sex make her Akhavan's clearest progenitor in deciding, contra some schools of cinefeminist thinking, that rather than avert her gaze from screening sex, she would instead turn on the high beams (see San Filippo 2020a, 165–350). "I want to learn more about the way people communicate through fucking, and that's what I want my films to do, too," Akhavan states (Northrup 2018, 23). Of course, it reveals much about the support (financial and otherwise) that women working to "fuck with the medium" could expect in the French versus the US contexts of independent filmmaking that it would take a decade for Breillat's challenging, courageous corpus to find American adherents able to engage anywhere as fully as her gaze-reorienting films do.

22 Appropriate Behavior

Figure 5
Homage through mise-en-scène: an image from Catherine Breillat's *Fat Girl* as the banner illustration on Akhavan's Twitter profile page.

By century's turn, the microbudget indie filmmaking facilitated by digital technologies had benefitted women filmmakers excluded from the Hollywood studio system, making it possible for a number of unproven talents to direct first features; I'll focus on two. Seattle-based Lynn Shelton was over forty when her first feature *We Go Way Back* (2006) was released, while Greta Gerwig was not yet twenty-five when she co-directed with Joe Swanberg *Nights and Weekends* (2008), on which the two also collaborated as writers and stars. Would that Shelton had not died unexpectedly in 2020, at only fifty-four years old, leaving us with eight quiet yet beautifully crafted films alongside television directing gigs, including the one that would win her a posthumous Emmy nomination, on the limited series *Little Fires Everywhere* (2020). At the precocious end of the age spectrum, Gerwig's early prominence in Mumblecore cinema led to high-profile Hollywood supporting roles that she subsequently leveraged for a return to directing with *Lady Bird* (2017), for which she became only the fifth woman ever to be nominated for best director.

Taking a brief detour from discussion of Akhavan's queer cohort, I view her in connection with Shelton and Gerwig because all three were part of, yet largely written out of, the Mumblecore legend that consecrated aughts American male filmmakers like Swanberg and the Duplass brothers and paved the way for their subsequent prominence as indie incubators. Having voiced an early claim to recuperate these and other women's authorial roles within Mumblecore's history, Claire Perkins's aforementioned study of Akhavan's in-betweenness additionally notes the diversity Akhavan brought into an otherwise straight male sensibility, aptly summing up *Appropriate Behavior* as "transpos[ing] the emotional awkwardness of mumblecore from the terms of male anxiety and egotism to those of a queer female subjectivity" (2016, 150). Born within a year of Gerwig, Akhavan's equally precocious entry into directing by way of her co-created web series places her within Mumblecore's second generation; she cites Swanberg's *Hannah Takes the Stairs* (2007), starring Gerwig and their mutual collaborator Mark Duplass, as "the first time I'd seen a film that was lower budget" (Wickham 2015). This indie film ecosystem, one nourished by support from leading US festivals Sundance and South by Southwest, served as Akhavan's practical model and primary motivator for her feature debut – more so than NYU's graduate film program (where, she recalls, "I didn't believe in my taste for a little while there" [Ehrlich 2015]) or even the US queer film scene, depleted as it was by the late aughts.

After *The Kids Are All Right*, the next lesbian-centred crossover success (in terms of both prominence and profits) would come from abroad and cause even greater controversy. Whereas Cholodenko's middle-aged lesbians were criticized for their mundane love life, *Blue Is the Warmest Color* (2013) elicited indignation for going to the opposite extreme with its ostensibly overlong sex scenes, perceived as porn-inspired leering by its straight male director. Akhavan herself has expressed her scorn for the film, even taking to her Twitter account in 2017 to call out *IndieWire* for putting the film at the top of its "Best Sex Scenes of the 21st Century" listicle (Akhavan 2017). However much the film invites a distanced critical appraisal of its often-unsettling lesbian representation, the irony it elicits is hardly comedic. And, as I note elsewhere, our assessment of and investments in the film must be reassessed in the wake of revelations about on-set abuses, as well as disparagement of the screen adaptation by the lesbian graphic novelist who authored the source material (San Filippo 2020a, 1–27). Yet this enduringly provocative film sparked early rumblings of what would coalesce into the #MeToo Movement, and thus provoked a pendulum swing that revalidated the importance of authenticity and sensitivity in screening women's and queer bodies and intimacies – an important context for *Appropriate Behavior*'s premiere just sixteen months later. Shortly thereafter, Akhavan would be among those movie industry figures invited in 2019 to join the Academy of Motion Picture Arts and Sciences in an overdue effort to diversify its ranks. Thereupon her entry into the pantheon of feminist auteurs became official, having also received the imprimatur, by the cinefeminist company Girls on Tops, of a tee-shirt bearing her name. "They're cheapening their brand!," was her self-deprecating response.

However belated and co-opted by Hollywood and capitalism it was, this wellspring of #MeToo-era awareness and activism has provoked industry-wide change unprecedented since the women's liberation movement. In retrospect, it may have been fortuitous that Akhavan put the brakes on developing *Appropriate Behavior* when her producer–creative partner Cecilia Frugiuele proposed giving her a year to raise funding for a slightly less penu-

Figure 6
Consecrated, and commodified, as a feminist auteur with a commemorative shirt created by cine-feminist company Girls on Tops.

rious production, and later when its earliest submissions for film festivals were unsuccessful. By the time *Appropriate Behavior* found its way into the world, the cultural climate awaiting women filmmakers had become more welcoming. And yet there was another obstacle to contend with in the throng of indie films, as Geoff King describes them, "cannibalizing each other's markets" (2014, 7). Having glimpsed that crowded playing field while at NYU, Akhavan intuited an alternative route into filmmaking – and in the process formed her first life-changing creative partnership. This breakout project had her team up with then classmate/girlfriend Ingrid Jungermann to make a web series set among, and named for, the lesbian bourgeoisie of Park Slope, Brooklyn …

"Talking Smack about Gay People"

Coming after the iconic soap *The L Word* (2004–09) but before *Orange Is the New Black* (2013–19), *The Slope* spoke to viewers dissatisfied with crossover content like *Glee* (2009–15) and *Modern Family* (2009–20), works designed to target "quality" LGBTQ+ audiences without sacrificing broad appeal (Ng 2013, 258–83; Himberg 2014, 289–304). Rejecting the compromises inherent in addressing mainstream audiences, emergent queer creators in the late 2000s and early 2010s gravitated to the freedom offered in the web-based realm of what was becoming known as "indie TV." The affordability and ease of web series production, combined with the proliferation of video-hosting sites like YouTube and Vimeo and crowd-funding mechanisms like Kickstarter and Patreon, encouraged risk-taking, uncompromising ventures designed for niche viewership.

In his 2018 book *Open TV*, Aymar Jean Christian places the web series as a preeminent mode of 2000s–10s indie content creation, having earlier credited it with "model[ing] the kind of open, and diverse, TV ecosystem the deregulated landscape was intended to fertilize, before corporations purchased distribution channels, increasing the scale of production but not always wages, creative freedom or audience and brand input" (Christian 2014, 161; see also Christian 2018). Though this first generation of web series found few avenues for monetization – *The Slope* is still available for free viewing, as it always has been – its promise as a launching pad into film festivals, feature filmmaking, cable TV development deals, and production/distribution partnerships with specialty outlets like Comedy Central, IFC, and LOGO turned into longer-term profits. This "open TV" renaissance would prove especially generative for queer women and/or women of colour, offering to many a stepping-stone into the ranks of media creators and, eventually, filmmakers and showrunners: from Issa Rae (*Misadventures of Awkward Black Girl*; *Insecure*) to Abbi Jacobson and Ilana Glazer (*Broad City*) to Katja Blichfeld (*High Maintenance*) to Fatimah Asghar and Sam Bailey (*Brown Girls*) to Linda Yvette Chávez (*Gentefied*). In its first generation the web series seemed to offer an edgier, less filtered version of LGBTQ+ representation than legacy TV afforded, one that Akhavan recalls "could be anything I wanted it to be. I'd seen so many films that I had such a clear idea of what a good film looked like, but with a webseries, it was like, make your own genre up – it was so much freedom, and you decide what's good ... I really didn't give a shit what was proper or right. If I hadn't made the webseries I would never have been able to make a film like [*Appropriate Behavior*] that's kind of outside the box" (Ward 2014).

From the vantage point of 2021, with vertical reintegration underway within the movie business and behemoths Netflix and Amazon leading an industry-wide consolidation that entertainment analyst Matt Stoller (2019) calls "Concentration Creep," the open TV era appears at its end. The industry's voracious appetite for streaming content has opened up opportunities, but at the same time threatens the outsiderdom that enabled the indie web series to flourish. Though the increased availability of development and licensing deals is understandably an appealing prospect for creators, it may prove a Faustian bargain – not simply in terms of sacrificing creative control, but also in the merciless workings of the streaming economy. Able to demand exclusive distribution rights for original or even licensed content, and having amassed enormous libraries, these streaming giants ruthlessly cancel even popular shows before contract renewals and back-end payouts raise production costs, assured of a well-nigh limitless reserve army of content to serve up to subscribers.

Akhavan's emergence on the scene in 2010, then, the year that she and Jungermann debuted their two-season web series *The Slope*, was well-timed. What started as a class assignment for NYU professor and filmmaker Ira Sachs's course – as Akhavan described it, "What if we filmed us talking smack about gay people?" (Dawson 2015) – developed into a vanguard work of LGBTQ+ cultural production, one that pioneered a new breed of defiantly irreverent, slyly ironic web series that emerged in the early 2010s. Revisiting *The Slope*, however briefly, serves importantly to introduce and underscore its significance in premiering the alter-ego persona that Akhavan would go on to perfect in *Appropriate Behavior*. As significant as Sundance's support and a provocative premise were for enabling *Appropriate Behavior*'s success, Akhavan's already acquired fan base was equally important.

Encouraged by the amused response of their classmates and egged on by Sachs (who would become a mentor to both women), Akhavan and Jungermann went on to make two seasons of eight episodes apiece, which they self-released on the video-hosting site Vimeo between 2010 and 2012. *The Slope* found patronage from alt-comedy impresario Michael Showalter (another of their NYU professors, who would guest star in one episode) as well as crowd-sourced financing for season 2. In 2012, Akhavan and Jungermann were named among *Filmmaker*'s 25 New Faces of Independent Film and appeared on LGBTQ+ monthly *Out*'s annual Out100 list, accolades that preview how their subsequent careers would forge a coalition between independent and LGBTQ+ entertainment industry niches and audience sensibilities (Dawson 2012; Out.com Editors 2012). As the second season fictionally chronicled, the series' end coincided with their relationship's breakup – a subject to which both would return in their first features: for Jungermann, the 2016 dark comedy *Women Who Kill*; for Akhavan, *Appropriate Behavior*.

Through the safe remove of their (as the tagline warned) "superficial, homophobic" alter egos, Akhavan and Jungermann play exaggerated versions of themselves. To watch *The Slope*'s debut episode ("Miserable Animals"), in which they dispute whether Desiree, as a bisexual, can rightfully refer to her girlfriend Ingrid as "super-dykey," stages the same drama of community infighting over language that Akhavan relates wrestling with in her comments on *Fresh Air*, quoted at the start of act I. Defending herself against Ingrid's disapproval at her attempted reclaiming of the slur, Desiree offers a more radically queer (if self-serving) conceptualization of language as unfixed, contingent (on both speaker and audience), and available for appropriation. The episode grants victory to neither position – clearly one-upping each other was more important to both than deciding the question – but as in all subsequent episodes their bickering odd-couple routine casts twenty-something Akhavan in the roles of campy queen, flighty bisexual, and (when it suits her motives, as above) more-woke-than-thou Millennial to thirty-something Jungermann's more grouchy, old-school lesbian. For every self-directed jab, Akhavan and Jungermann land another to the collective thorax of so-called PC culture. The result questions the assumptions underlying queer discursive politics and discourse-policing more generally, all while nimbly balancing on the knife edge of causing offence, even outrage, through recourse to the ironic distancing provided by their self-professedly "superficial, homophobic" alter-ego articulations of what Jungermann and Akhavan respectively would later describe, in echoing terms, as the "things I think and am afraid to say" (Dry 2015) and "the stuff that we're uncomfortable to say out loud" (Stanford 2018).

In a 2012 profile of the partners on queer women's media site AfterEllen, Akhavan pleads with fans to spread the word about *The Slope* for fear that otherwise "we are all going to be stuck with Whitney from *The Real L Word* [2010–12] as the voice of our people" (Bendix 2012). Referring to the most noxious character in the widely reviled reality spin-off series, Akhavan's snarky warning functions as oppositional branding. Singling out *The Real L Word* for further derision in the season 1 episode "Queer Programming," Ingrid resists Desiree's entreaties to view the show: "I don't even like that it exists. I'm not going to watch an episode." Desiree responds, "I don't like it either but I'm obligated to watch because it's the only queer programming." The sound emitted by Desiree's cell phone a moment later reveals that her ringtone is *The L Word*'s opening credits track. With this debate over the lose-lose alternatives of avoiding or indulging in pandering programming, *The Slope* slyly promotes its own niche-filling potential as a superior alternative. Much like another citation that would make its way into *Appropriate Behavior*, in the scene of a stoned Shirin protesting of (gay camp favourite) *Sex and the City* (1998–2004), "You've got to admit it's pretty fucking entertaining," only to have Maxine stubbornly pronounce it "boring," the dual concession to and derision for the "bad objects" of mainstream queer content locate its creators along the same lineage but as edgier outliers to *The L Word*'s mainstream prominence within twenty-first-century queer women's television.

Upping the stakes from gay TV's guilty pleasures to LGBTQ+ youth activism, *The Slope*'s fifth episode parodies the It Gets Better public service announcement series co-founded by sex educator Dan Savage to offer supportive queer testimonies. Titled "It Gets Better?," Desiree and Ingrid's sardonic entry into the viral video campaign offers a camp retort to its sanctimonious, often overwrought address. As Ingrid notes, "Not only are they really dramatic, they're not really helpful." Proposing a more practical approach, Ingrid admits to having evaded youthful bullying, saying, "I wasn't out in high school. I mostly dated athletic black men." Desiree confesses she was "most definitely" bullied, not because of her sexuality but "because I was very ugly, and a little bit fat … Nobody really gave a shit about my sexuality." She concludes, "There is a way to be out, gay and happy in high school and it's if you are a hot girl." "Or a colorful gay guy that has a boa and a catchphrase," Ingrid adds. In relating their own experiences in terms that counter the dominant script, the couple challenges the It Gets Better campaign's characterization of high school politics as grounded in heteronormativity – suggesting rather that factors such as social affiliation, athleticism, lookism, and charisma may matter more. They present a checklist as a substitute for the "vague advice" they find the campaign disseminating, "for kids who want to *make* things better" (with tenets ranging from "Don't be fat" to "Don't do theatre"). The video ends with a final admonition from Desiree, spoken with a sassy inflection that emphasizes its tongue-in-cheek deflation of both self-dramatizing gay youth alongside the It Gets Better campaign's inducements to them: "Don't kill yourself, because suicide is super gay."

Like the lesbian Statler and Waldorf (of *Muppets* fame), these cantankerous hecklers of queer histrionics deliver snarky dismissals of positivity, pride, and most things homonormative – from *The L Word* to It Gets Better

Figure 7
Tongue in cheek activism: Ingrid and Desiree's "It Gets Better?" video pokes fun at queer drama.

– so as to challenge the commodification of queerness and the containment of its disruptive potential. As Jack Halberstam describes this approach (though not addressing Akhavan and Jungermann specifically), "In this work, a queer aesthetic is activated through the function of negation rather than in the mode of positivity; in other words, the works strive to establish queerness as a mode of critique rather than as a new investment in normativity or life or respectability or wholeness or legitimacy" (2011, 110–11). *The Slope*'s (self-)satire targets not only the homonormative impulse that drives everything from *The L Word* (and its ambivalent fandom) to It Gets Better, but also the broader bourgeois community formations that Akhavan finds herself always displaced from on account of (as she characterized Shirin) always "feel[ing] inappropriate."

Even in its milder moments, however, *The Slope* manifests what literary theorist Linda Hutcheon describes as irony's "unbearable slipperiness," which makes it, as a tool of counter-discourse, a "highly unstable one, sometimes even a dangerous one" in its "transideological" malleability and interpretability (1995, 196). In her 2017 book *Kill All Normies*, Angela Nagle traces how the rise of the alt-right has tactically co-opted and weaponized irony for reactionary political purposes. Even if one dissents from Nagle's diagnosis of liberal virtue-signalling as both motive and means for the alt-right's growth in numbers and power, it seems prudent for both artist and critic to reassess such artworks to gauge how their humour now lands. Timing, after all, is comedy's most crucial element.

As Akhavan mentions in the interview that concludes this book, there is one joking line within *Appropriate Behavior* she now sees as problematic, but she finds the humour in *The Slope* worth defending for the way it punches up rather than down – that is, the target (when not themselves) has equivalent or more cultural privilege than the humorists. The humour furthermore emanates from lived queer identity and experience and is intended primarily for a like-minded, in-the-know audience inhabiting the same marginalized segment of society, about whom it attempts to speak truthfully rather than in the "cliché" that no one, most of all Akhavan or her onscreen alter egos, can live up to. Yet, while in 2015 Akhavan readily admitted "I'm very politically incorrect and always have been," my questioning her in 2020 (in the interview that follows) about whether she would still describe herself that way received a thoughtful pause followed by "No." My sense is that it's the societal stakes, rather than Akhavan's contrarian sensibility, that have changed; whereas the era of Obama and *Obergefell*[5] allowed for a fractionalized self-questioning and mocking meta-commentary within LGBTQ+ community cultures, in the intervening years – particularly the dark days of summer 2020 when our discussion took place – that energy needed to be directed outward and against the forces of reaction, and better put to coalition-building with other oppressed groups.

That said, irony is not inherently apolitical nor should it be abandoned as a strategy only because it has become the preferred tool of toxic agents. In reflecting on *Appropriate Behavior*, I am reminded of what Jeffrey Sconce terms the "smart film," the creation of 1990s indie auteurs such as Noah Baumbach, David O. Russell, and Todd Solondz. Sconce characterizes their work by its opposition to mainstream cinema and its attendant value system, an opposition achieved by "experimenting with *tone* as a means of critiquing 'bourgeois' taste and culture" (2002, 352, original emphasis). Defending such films as *Kicking and Screaming* (1995), *Spanking the Monkey* (1994), and *Happiness* (1998) against critics who saw their ironic detachment as infected by (in film critic Manohla Dargis's words) "the new nihilism," Sconce argued against the perception that irony is incompatible with ideological commitment: "In its refusal of conventional terms of debate, irony can be a brutally honest rhetorical strategy ... a strategic disengagement from a certain terrain of belief, politics and commitment" (269). The ironic disengagement of Sconce's smart films conveyed their critique of mainstream culture and the bourgeois values it embodies, even as their irony expresses "the futility of pure politics or absolute morality" (368). In my own reassessment, nearly a decade on, of *The Slope* and *Appropriate Behavior*, I see both as latter-day smart films, particularly in their opposition to their mainstream or Hollywood-style analogues, whether of queer television programming or romantic comedy. Much as Sconce sees tone working in 1990s smart films, their pronounced affectlessness – "dry" and "deadpan" are two adjectives frequently applied to Akhavan and Jungermann's work – communicates their disdain of and disengagement from cultural norms and bourgeois values, even as they reveal their hypocrisy and privileged self-regard as the very means by which they and we can appreciate the humour. Though Sconce's article fails to mention a single woman auteur, there were at the time of his writing women making smart films, Nicole Holofcener for one, and since then women auteurs have increasingly gained the cultural privilege to provoke with the caustic charm that has long been the province of male auteurs, as evidenced by such work as Phoebe Waller-Bridge's *Fleabag* (2016–19), Michaela Coel's *I May Destroy You* (2020), and Emerald Fennell's *Promising Young Woman* (2020).

To consider, writing in 2021, that *The Slope* premiered just a decade ago attests both to the rapid ascendancy of Akhavan's career, but also to how radically the public discourse has changed in the intervening decade. From the perspective of circa-2021 "cancel culture" some of *The Slope*'s humour seems genuinely shocking, but even at the time it seemed unsurprising that it failed to achieve the legacy TV adaptation awarded contemporaneous breakout web series *Broad City* (2010–11, 2014–19), *High Maintenance* (2012–15, 2016–20), and *Misadventures of Awkward Black Girl* (2011; [as *Insecure*] 2016–21). Yet it paved the way for Akhavan and Jungermann's first features, as well as a veritable cottage industry of similarly snarky web series – including Jungermann's own sophomore effort, the acclaimed *F to 7th* (2013–14). While the notice and experience that came with making *The Slope* was undeniably a springboard for *Appropriate Behavior*, equally inspiring, if hard-hitting, to both was their unpartnering ...

"The Best Enabler"

The Slope ends where *Appropriate Behavior* begins: with the dissolution of a relationship. The series finale, titled "Miserable Best Friends Who Used to Be Together," looks backward to the first episode ("Miserable Animals") both in its title and in returning the couple to the scene of their earlier fight, ostensibly to determine custody of their dog – a stray who, having wandered up in that opening episode, initiated their squabbling over what Desiree viewed as Ingrid's "super-dykey" instinct to nurture. The finale also looks forward, to *Appropriate Behavior*'s riffing off the breakup ur-text *Annie Hall*, with its pessimistic protagonist's division of the world into "the horrible and the miserable." Even as we mourn the passing of the irreverent comedy generated by Ingrid and Desiree's mutual misanthropy – as Desiree puts it, "a shared disregard for social norms and common human decency is a terrible thing to waste" – their uncoupling proves still more generative, both for deepening *The Slope*'s dramatic pathos and for propelling the couple into their solo creative ventures. While their constant onscreen bickering sends them in circles of what Ingrid characterizes as "fighting about fighting" – "I don't think we fight that much," protests Desiree in response, obliviously – the ex-couple's far more productive route has been to rewrite their relationship's script by means of creating new work. Though (and perhaps through) parodying onscreen their own ambivalent inertia and self-delusion, the real-life couple moved past the difficult early stages of breaking up.

In weaving together the fictional and non-fictional, the personal and the professional, the uncoupling narrative becomes the vehicle through which both women seek, and attain, autobiographical agency in the form of creative control. As Akhavan (2015b) recalls of the breakup, "I felt out of control when events were happening and I didn't get to call the shots and this is what I do to be in control. If my heart's broken then I can gain control of that narrative." Self-serving as it may be, this repurposing of their past relationship into creative production as practised by both Akhavan and Jungermann is grounded in growth rather than regression or revenge. In my longer study (2019, 991–1008) of the ex-couple's co-created and post-collaborative work, I make the case that by resignifying their relationship's ostensible "failure" as instead generative of positive transformation both personal and professional, Akhavan and Jungermann reconceive what constitutes success, whether in love or elsewhere in life. As I argue, there is radically queer potential therein: for in converting their former romantic and erotic attachments into creative investments, the ex-couple defies masculinist and monogamist models of individualist authorship and proprietary coupling.

In modelling a queer-feminist *praxis* – a theory-based creative practice – Akhavan's and Jungermann's respective uncoupling narratives participate in a larger historical turn within queer studies that emphasizes the reparative potential of retrospection: a returning to, so as to reckon with, loss and trauma.

Envisioned as a hopeful, productive mode of queer oppositionality, this praxis urges the (re)claiming of cultural texts and artifacts that, Jack Halberstam describes, "refuse triumphalist accounts of gay, lesbian, [bisexual[6]] and transgender history" and so reject a heteronormative and homonormative "logic of achievement, fulfillment, and success(ion)" (2011, 23, 94). Clearly resonant for an LGBTQ+ community defined into existence and sustained through exclusion, persecution, and plague, this "reparative return" offers a route to individual healing as well. It is challenging not to think of Jungermann as the inspiration for Maxine – and Akhavan as the inspiration for either/both of the love interests, one Iranian American and the other bisexual, of protagonist Morgan (played by Jungermann) in *Women Who Kill* – much as it is difficult to distinguish between *Annie Hall*'s central couple Alvy and Annie and the performers who play them, ex-couple Woody Allen and Diane Keaton (née Hall).

A similarly inspiring example of women's creative collaboration can be found in that of Akhavan and Italian-born, UK-based writer-producer Cecilia Frugiuele, whom Akhavan calls "my partner in all things except the romantic" (SBS Staff 2019). Having met at the University of London (where Akhavan spent a year studying abroad), their friendship perhaps provided inspiration in part for that in *The Bisexual* between Akhavan's character Leila and close friend Deniz (Saskia Chana), who also meet there, and assuredly inspired Akhavan's impetuous move back to the city in 2015. In her *Fresh Air* interview, Akhavan shared her sense of both their relationship's and her relocation's significance in saying: "Living near her is the best enabler. So it's been really great being close to the person in life who motivates you and believes in you. She always would like me to clarify that we're not romantic partners. I talk about her as though she's my wife. But she is, you know, one of the loves of my life" (Akhavan and Danforth 2018). As this winding journey through *Appropriate Behavior*'s protracted production history attests, the DIY model for media creation necessitates enormous individual labour, investment, and risk; creative partnerships between women are indispensable foundations for queer-feminist artmaking and activism broadly, and for Akhavan's career specifically. Act II will look at another platonic coupling within *Appropriate Behavior*, that between Shirin and her best pal Crystal, as similarly inspired by the friendship between Akhavan and the actor playing opposite her, "oldest friend" (Ehrlich 2014) and playwright-performer Halley Feiffer.

"The Next Lena Dunham"

In the flurry of headlines and soundbites so describing Akhavan upon *Appropriate Behavior*'s premiere, it went overlooked that it was Akhavan herself who first publicly noted that Dunham's success could either propel or imperil her own (see Setoodeh 2014). In her 2013 screed "Who Wrote It Better?," Akhavan confessed her fears that the *Girls* (2012–17) creator's ascendant star meant "my work is not safe – my potential career is in jeopardy. We're too damn similar and she beat me to the punch." The piece is flattering of Dunham and flip throughout – signing off "that said, thank god she's not Iranian or bisexual otherwise I'd have to cut her" – yet reflects Akhavan's genuine recognition of the cultural imperative to position women celebrities as competitors (Akhavan 2013). Very much opposed, then, to the collaborative model of queer-feminist praxis described above, this pigeonholing devalues – figuratively and literally – female artists through comparisons that conflate and deindividuate their accomplishments, serving as an implicit warning that, as Akhavan expresses, "There's no room for more than one woman whose work can be monetized ... That's ridiculous, I've never read about my male contemporaries that they're the next Noah Baumbach" (Ward 2015). That the moniker, taken up by critics and culture beat writers, would mutate further into "the Iranian, bisexual Lena Dunham" is all too predictable, yet as this book's finale will take up, Akhavan spun that cliché into creative gold when she drew on the designation as her inspiration for *The Bisexual*. Having provided *Appropriate Behavior* its best blurb, Dunham cast Akhavan in a three-episode arc during

Figure 8
Hannah (Lena Dunham) reading her autofiction as classmate Chandra (Desiree Akhavan) listens in the fourth season of *Girls*.

Girls' fourth season in which their characters take turns one-upping each other at the esteemed Iowa Writers' Workshop – undoubtedly encouraging the comparisons, yet also communicating their mutual admiration, and presenting an endearingly knowing depiction of their shared affinity for irony-inflected self-exhibitionism. Even as we resist reductively pairing them as a means of marketing shorthand, we can acknowledge the real parallels between them. Both mine laughs by mocking a more naïvely self-important, ego-unbridled version of herself. Both are willing to appear naked or unflatteringly attired on-screen. Told by an audience member following an *Appropriate Behavior* screening at the Provincetown festival in 2014 that she was brave, Akhavan recalls, "I thought he was saying I was brave for being an Iranian bisexual. But he said, 'You have the smallest tits ever, but you show them, and I think

Figure 9
Shirin models the "grown-up underwear of a woman in charge of her sexuality and not afraid of change."

we need to see different kinds of breasts in movies.' I couldn't stop laughing, but I said, 'You're right, and I'm starting a revolution'" (Kachka 2015).

With tongue-in-cheek reference to Akhavan's own participation in such postfeminist strategies of self-empowerment, one of *Appropriate Behavior*'s most slyly funny scenes shows a post-breakup Shirin shopping for new underwear – Maxine having vengefully cut hers up – in an upscale lingerie boutique with pal Crystal, who exclaims over a wispy accessory for sale, "Who spends three hundred dollars on a garter belt?" Attracting the attention of the store's steely proprietress, Shirin demurs that her diminutive measurements make wearing a bra seem "a little silly. You know, like little girls who carry purses," only to be informed with utmost seriousness, "Just because your breasts are small doesn't mean they aren't legitimate." Carried along, Shirin concurs, "You know, it's like I didn't think I deserved a bra, because I didn't see myself as a real woman." The ensuing sight-gag, in which an absurdly attired Shirin, goaded into trying on a pink corset, emerges from the dressing room to have the proprietress pronounce her "stunning" as an incredulous Crystal looks on, is – in contrast with the merchandise – priceless.

Akhavan brazenly bares still more of her small-breasted self and of her gift for cringe-inducing sexual realism in the scene in which Shirin embarks on a threesome with a couple who pick her up in a bar. Arriving back at their place, her host Marie offers to model her latex outfit, saying enticingly, "I have to oil it to put it on." The libidinous mood shifts almost immediately, however, thanks to Shirin's guffaw when Marie's boyfriend Ted announces, "I have a latex outfit too." Though Ted clearly takes offence, things progress once the latex-clad Marie appears; cut to Shirin, going down on Marie until she orgasms exuberantly. Yet the afterglow soon gives way to awkwardness, as the couple's familiar embrace seems to catch Shirin out – quite literally, this being the moment that yields the image used in the film's marketing and that graces this book's cover. As Catherine McDermott perceptively notes of the cinematography here, "[Shirin] cannot disappear into the moment, as Ted and Marie do; therefore she remains acutely in focus" (2018, 113). Things go swiftly downhill, with Shirin and Ted failing to muster the necessary chemistry. The scene is all the more excruciating yet impressive for its duration and lack of dialogue – Shirin and Ted signal their mutual distaste through the subtlest of gestures and glances. After some half-hearted fumbling, Ted extricates himself and sullenly leaves the women alone, whereupon Shirin apologizes for having "gotten in my head." Continuing to talk, the women find their sexual rapport shift into something sweeter but still sufficiently charged to rattle Ted, who returns to the room and stands stiffly by as Shirin rises to dress and heads out, the two women saying a forlorn farewell.

Showing how sexual adventure can swiftly sober into uncomfortable reality, this sequence showcases Akhavan's talent for handling sex scenes, calibrated precisely so as to be persuasively passionate one moment, tipping into extreme awkwardness the next, and seeming all the more authentic for it. The same tact characterizes her subsequent work, as comparable scenes in *The Miseducation of Cameron Post* (2018) and *The Bisexual* indicate. Of the threesome scene, Akhavan recalls, "I'm simulating oral sex, but I never felt uncomfortable because I knew I was at the helm of the ship. I felt so empowered. I knew I was going to be in the editing room, that I could take any risk I wanted to take, and that I could cut it out if I didn't think it was appropriate" (Wickham 2015). Akhavan indicates here how the shaping of such scenes, in a departure from her typical modus operandi, calls for what's "appropriate" to be respected rather than transgressed. Her career having shared a timeline with the #MeToo movement and the introduction of intimacy coordinators onto film and television production sets, Akhavan's approach to screening sex establishes a valuable precedent for remaining "appropriate" without, as Shirin will accuse Maxine of doing during a failed attempt at role play, "killing the sexy."

To draw a last connection between Akhavan and Dunham, their shared penchant for bodily and sexual mortification in their onscreen personas derives its authenticity from experience, as borne out through each woman's testimony. Far be it for Akhavan to feign having been eternally cool or always in possession of her now striking looks; as she has often recounted to the press, at age fourteen she was voted ugliest girl in school by her peers. To Terry Gross's disbelief at hearing this on *Fresh Air*, Akhavan replied: "I'm someone who grew into my face. I legit was an uncomfortable-looking kid. The Beast was my nickname. I'm very tall. I'm 5′11″ and 190 pounds at that age and just did not fit into what an attractive girl at [New York prep school] Horace Mann should look like" (Akhavan and Danforth 2018). Akhavan's honesty in recalling this painful treatment and discomfort with her looks and body image – which in her teens and twenties found her acquiescing to rhinoplasty and entering rehab for treatment of bulimia – finds voice through her characters, whether in Shirin referring to herself as "a Before model for Accutane" or in *The Bisexual*'s Leila's explanation to a friend surprised that she didn't have sex in her teen years. "Did you grow up religious?" the friend asks; "No, I grew up ugly!" Leila responds.[7] Much like the truth to be mined from showing the awkward alongside the arousing in sex scenes, these allusions to Akhavan's ugly duckling adolescence brings to her work a humorous yet unsparing appraisal of the lookism by which women's value continues to be assessed. Yet in turning now to explore how the reparative riches of revisiting a painful breakup resulted in her feature debut, it bears quoting Akhavan's recollection of her reward for having set her sights, and therefore her sense of self-worth, elsewhere: "Having the opportunity to shoot your first feature must be what getting married is like for a certain type of woman. After so many years of fantasizing and months of preparation, it was a beautiful, emotional, and life-affirming experience that was over much too quickly and evoked instant nostalgia" (Akhavan 2013).

Act II
"A Gay *Annie Hall*"

> I really love *Annie Hall* ... It was the first film I saw that was a love story about a couple that was doomed from the start. The first line of the film is "Well, Annie and I broke up." You know the premise, you know it's not going to work out, and yet the challenge of the film that it succeeds in is [getting you to] somehow fall in love with this couple, rooting for them, and yet kind of understanding why they can't stay together. And it was that challenge that I wanted to set for myself going into [*Appropriate Behavior*].
> Desiree Akhavan at the BFI National Archive

"A Nervous Romance"

If act I began with the perhaps audacious claim that a film released in 2014 deserves recognition as a queer film *classic*, act II also (dare I say) inappropriately commences with Akhavan's own callout to a film indelibly associated with its co-creator Woody Allen, whose lustre has dimmed considerably due to ongoing personal scandals and an oeuvre that despite its steady output has for decades produced more misses than hits. Allen's 1977 comedy *Annie Hall* remains his most critically acclaimed (regularly turning up on "best of" lists) and most commercially successful work (Lauria 2013).[1] While not as massively crowd-pleasing as that era's blockbuster comedies *Blazing Saddles* (1974) and *Airplane!* (1981), *Annie Hall* proved sufficiently popular and widely praised that it swept that year's Academy Awards, receiving four of the five top honours and becoming one of only a handful of comedies awarded Best Picture (famously beating out *Star Wars*). To my mind its more impressive claim to distinction, and a source of its enduring importance, was signalled by its original tagline: "A nervous romance." Disrupting Hollywood's history of debonair pairings and "happily ever afters" to depict emotional entanglement between socially awkward neurotics who are (as Akhavan says) "doomed from the start," *Annie Hall* marked a turning point in the romantic comedy genre, a film groundbreaking in its narrative and formal rupturing of romcom and cinematic conventions alike.

Tamar Jeffers McDonald, a leading scholar of romantic comedy, singles out *Annie Hall* as exemplifying what she names "radical romantic comedy," the brief period when the genre abandoned fantasy wish-fulfillment to engage in skeptical questioning of the regime of heteronormative coupling; radical romcoms so frequently failed to deliver the expected couple (re)formation that a veritable subgenre of "uncoupling comedies" emerged (2007, 59–84).[2] Stemming from cultural and industrial shake-ups of the 1960s and '70s – women's lib, the sexual revolution, the loosening of censorship restrictions – romcom faced challenges to its bedrock values that had some film critics (most famously Brian Henderson) prematurely predicting its demise (1978, 11–23). Instead, romcom absorbed the shock, gaining vitality by modernizing in both ideological and aesthetic senses. Hollywood would eventually retreat back into making what's been called neo-traditional romcom, churning out Cinderella-style fairy tales–cum–commercial hits stretching from *Pretty Woman* (1990) to *Enchanted* (2007), and beyond. But in the anomalous era that was 1970s Hollywood, studios released such boundary-pushing products as the swingers sex comedy *Bob & Carol & Ted & Alice* (1969) and *Harold and Maude* (1971), an offbeat May-December romance between a septuagenarian Holocaust survivor and a death-obsessed post-adolescent. Accordingly, *Annie*

Hall in its opening monologue overturns romcom's "boy meets girl, boy loses girl, boy gets girl" formula and then proceeds, in the course of its ninety-three-minute runtime, to skeptically question our compulsive quest for romantic relationships ("You know, they're totally irrational and crazy and absurd") only ultimately to conclude, as the joke goes, "We need the eggs."

Allen's career highpoint is the consummate example not only of radical romcom's narrative reinvention and ideological revision, but of its aesthetic rejuvenation as well. Two decades earlier *Pillow Talk* (1959) had played, rather hammily, with split screen as a means to imply sexual impropriety between leads Doris Day and Rock Hudson, and earlier still Ernst Lubitsch earned his moniker "Director of Doors" by cleverly gesturing to what was happening in the bedrooms behind them. But romcom got a stylistic jolt starting in 1967 with Mike Nichols's inspired use of asynchronous audio and incongruous soundtrack in *The Graduate* (see Stevens 2015, 85–112), which also left viewers with the most memorably unsettling open ending of any Hollywood movie up to that point. Where romcom style and content conventionally operate in tandem to reinforce the genre's mythologizing of romance – deploying soaring music and swooning camerawork to communicate the joy of a closing clinch – radical romcom's demythologizing renders its diegetic world disjointed and disillusioned. With *Annie Hall*, Allen pushed romcom's aesthetic innovation to a deconstructionist peak, cleverly marrying form and content by employing what Frank Krutnik describes as denarrativizing devices and Brechtian distanciation effects (1998, 15–36) – all those memorable, much-lauded uses of direct address, split screen, and surrealist transitions (courtesy of co-editors Ralph Rosenblum and Wendy Greene Bricmont) that exposed the impossibility of the romantic illusions the film wistfully grieved rather than wishfully embraced.

For a film to court comparison to *Annie Hall*, then, sets a high bar. And just as her designation by critics and culture beat writers as "the next Lena Dunham" originated with Akhavan herself, it was she who termed her debut feature *Annie Hall*–esque while it was still in the script development stage.

Profiled along with (by that time) ex-girlfriend Jungermann as two of *Filmmaker*'s 25 New Faces of 2012, Akhavan describes working on "a gay *Annie Hall*, with us as the leads, looking at the course of our relationship, with the same dynamics, from beginning to end" (Dawson 2012). Having the chutzpah to link her debut feature to Allen's finest but also the humility to acknowledge that doing so makes for convenient shorthand, Akhavan was setting herself up to be asked about Allen at every turn, as the epigraph above taken from the post-screening discussion at the British Film Institute attests. What Harold Bloom (1997 [1973]) famously termed "the anxiety of influence" proves particularly problematic in Allen's case, given the challenge of separating art from artist (what *New York Times* film critic A.O. Scott referred to in a 2018 piece as "My Woody Allen Problem"). As with many a conflicted fan, Akhavan's admiration for Allen's strongest work vies with (among other concerns) her exasperation at "all these pretty blonde white girls ... so honored to work with him [who] keep enabling him to make these shit films" (Akhavan 2015c; *Hollywood Reporter* Staff 2014).

In addition to calling out the homogeneity of Allen's leading ladies, Akhavan also turned the constant questioning about Allen's influence on *Appropriate Behavior* into a platform for protesting the sexist double standards that plague women directors. Act III considers how Akhavan faced down the "second film slump" reported by women filmmakers to follow even successful debuts. Denied the career momentum afforded by artistic and cultural capital of the sort Allen has long enjoyed, women filmmakers are understandably irked by the double standard Akhavan described in coming off *Appropriate Behavior*: "I don't think I have the luxury of making a B minus second film if I want to keep working, and I have seen male filmmakers make B minus movies and keep working. Who's going to finance the film after that? You go to director jail. Director jail is a place that exists and I don't wanna go there" (Akhavan 2015b). Akhavan here joins her voice to the growing protest throughout the industry against the myriad practices and inequities that have for so long disadvantaged women creators. The artistic adulation Allen long enjoyed despite three decades of critical and commercial disappointments and personal controversy speaks volumes about the enduring cult of the male auteur. However justified the critical consensus celebrating *Annie Hall*, one can sense this double standard at work when *Appropriate Behavior*, only seven minutes shorter, is assessed by the *Hollywood Reporter* upon release as "feel[ing] paper-thin even at just under 90 minutes. It's enjoyable but weightless" (Rooney 2014). Against this persistent belittlement of women-directed work, I find *Appropriate Behavior* making impressive use – comparable, in my view, to *Annie Hall* – of its economical runtime, packing comparable poignancy and profundity into what is (also like *Annie Hall*) only superficially a lightweight romantic comedy.

Heading to Park City in 2014, Akhavan was understandably wary of how the festival scene, and Sundance in particular, held comedies in low esteem; "Every year there's a film … that breaks through, and they're never comedies," she noted (Ehrlich 2014). Making matters worse, by 2014 a widely held perception regarding "the death of romcom" had taken hold, fuelled by media reports such as *L.A. Weekly* film critic Amy Nicholson's 2014 piece "Who Killed the Romantic Comedy?" Hitching her star to what was widely seen as either a trivial or a dying genre left Akhavan with even more to prove, particularly given that the critical disdain for romantic comedy is deeply connected to the genre's feminization, in terms of both audience and authorship. Though women directors and (especially) writers have achieved significantly greater success in romcom than in most other genres, even those who prosper (Nora Ephron, Nancy Meyers) are denied the prestige of their male counterparts who dominate more "masculine" genres. Understandably, some women creatives steer clear of romantic comedy, fearing that it will imperil their auteur credibility; as the esteemed Argentine filmmaker (and openly lesbian) Lucrecia Martel pronounced in 2018, "Romantic comedies are my enemy" (Hoberman 2018). In Martel's case, as in that of action movie maven Kathryn Bigelow (until 2021 the only woman awarded an Oscar for directing), this strategy has proven successful – Bigelow's sole work that fits the category of "women's film," her 2000 adaptation of Anita Shreve's *The Weight of Water*, was roundly panned and is downplayed in accounts of her career. Though their ability to get men into movie theatres accounts for the blockbuster success enjoyed by a handful of 2010s romcoms (*Bridesmaids*, 2011; *Magic Mike*, 2012; *Trainwreck*, 2015; *Girls Trip*, 2017; *Crazy Rich Asians*, 2018), in each instance a male director was reassuringly at the helm. Romcom's stigmatization is also reflected in a long tradition of critical and scholarly inattention or dismissal, that, as the case of Woody Allen again attests, it takes a male auteur to transcend.

Appearing at a time when the formulaic studio romcom seemed definitively to have collapsed into creative exhaustion, *Appropriate Behavior* revitalizes romcom as radically as did *Annie Hall* in its day. In appropriating an arguably feminist but not apparently queer film (we might speculate about Diane Keaton's masculine-tailored attire) to her own creative and critically queer ends, Akhavan ultimately outdoes Allen on multiple fronts. Updating Allen's Jew-WASP culture-clash uncoupling comedy to centre on a white lesbian and a bisexual woman of colour, Akhavan challenges romcom's rules of attraction by pushing a genre founded on straight white couple formation to adapt and innovate. Akhavan reorients the narrative towards the woman's perspective sidelined in *Annie Hall*, and trains her eye on a woman filmmaker's process of sexual and artistic self-formation by means of her protagonist and alter ego Shirin's struggle with both her sexual and professional identities. Revising *Annie Hall*'s script to critique Allen's, and by extension cinema's, indulgence of male egoism and artistic solipsism, Akhavan centres herself and makes her experience known. For these reasons I find it worth the risk she takes, and that I take as well in writing this, of summoning Allen's spirit, of perhaps even seeming to deflect the spotlight from *Appropriate Behavior* in swinging between it and *Annie Hall*. Like the best adaptations and sequels and remakes and re-imaginings, *Appropriate Behavior* borrows from its source to make something different and richer still.

"A Queer Romance"

In both *Annie Hall* and *Appropriate Behavior* the meet-cute occurs a third of the way into the film, well after the opening sequence has foretold the breakup to come.[3] *Appropriate Behavior*'s central couple meet on a Brooklyn stoop outside a New Year's Eve party, where Shirin's lack of political correctness as she sizes up Maxine (who wears a Keaton-esque tailored man's suit and Alvy-like black frames) both sparks their repartee and foreshadows the role it will play as a barrier to their long-term coupling.

SHIRIN: I love dykes.
MAXINE: You know that word is incredibly offensive.
SHIRIN: Oh, I'm bisexual so it's okay.
MAXINE: Still offensive.
SHIRIN: You know how I meant it.
MAXINE: Doesn't matter how you meant it.
SHIRIN: Tomato-tomahto.

Shirin's allusion to the Gershwin tune "Let's Call the Whole Thing Off," immortalized onscreen first by Astaire and Rogers and then by Harry and Sally, combines with the New Year's Eve timing to wink at romcom convention while announcing Akhavan's disruption of the (neo)traditional notion that opposites attract. Getting the final word without winning Maxine's acquiescence, Shirin's dismissal of their terminological dispute as trivial challenges Maxine's priggish insistence that context cannot recuperate traditionally homophobic language. This first meeting – and, tellingly, first fight – echoes the ones that begin and end *The Slope*, and resonates with ongoing debates among queer thinkers and media creators, including, as evidenced by the *Fresh Air* quotation that opens act I, Akhavan herself.

The meet-cute in *Annie Hall* memorably encompasses Annie's charmingly inane chattering ("La-di-da") and erratic driving followed, over drinks, by fatuous droning (on Alvy's part) and feigned self-composure (on Annie's). Their mutual desire to impress by suppressing their actual selves leaves so much unspoken that subtitling is needed to expose their unguarded interior monologues (Alvy: "I sound like FM radio ... she senses I'm shallow"; Annie: "I'm not smart enough for him"; Alvy: "I wonder what she looks like naked"). In comparison, Shirin and Maxine's is the more authentic exchange, in which the participants seem genuinely engaged with one another, even as they disagree, where Annie's oblivious microaggression in telling Alvy "You're what Grammy Hall would call a real Jew" elicits only an eye roll of disbelief in response. While cultural and, by extension, ideological division will prove as decisive a thorn in this couple's side as that between Alvy and Annie's Old and New Testament outlooks, at this early moment Maxine relents to a smile when Shirin continues, "I like girls like you. You know – manly, but also a little bit like a lady." "Nice, thank you," Maxine responds sarcastically, but shows herself to have softened further by acting unfazed when Shirin remarks about Maxine's ex, upon learning nothing more than that her name is Linda, "She sounds like a cunt." In casually dropping a term that carries equivalent potential to offend women as "dyke" does lesbians, Shirin cements her anti-PC stance and finds Maxine, for a time, a willing conspirator.

Soon further evidence that they are bound to bond emerges, as the pair discover their shared misanthropy. Swerving from furor over her ex to ranting about "Brooklyn parties and everyone talking about their Kickstarter campaigns," Maxine demands, "Did you see that guy with the waxed Dalí mustache? I mean, what the fuck is that guy's problem? Who the fuck does he think he is?" An enraptured Shirin responds, "I find your anger incredibly sexy. I hate so many things too." The kiss they exchange just shy of midnight, sealed by their common cynicism and distaste for the excesses of Millennial hipsterdom, counters romcom's valorization of screwball couples with their sunny comportment and playful camaraderie, along with their latter-day equivalents: manic pixie dream girls with their vacuous positivity and life-embracing out-

Figures 10–11
Queering the meet-cute: *Annie Hall* and *Appropriate Behavior*.

looks. The moment also winkingly references the real-life couple parodied in *The Slope*, the second season of which was Kickstarter-funded.

Shirin and Maxine's shared embrace of negativity establishes their (however short-term) compatibility. Post-breakup (but in the film's shuffled time scheme, a sequence that precedes the meet-cute), Shirin's attempt at sexual healing via a dating app turns up good-looking but vapid Henry (aka "BrooklynBoy82"). A close-up on his profile page, where his self-description begins "I like a lot of things," makes clear that Shirin's search for a casual encounter with the anti-Maxine is destined to disappoint. That those "things" include "good movies ... indie stuff, like Goddard [*sic*] and Tarentino [*sic*]," offers another sly jab at both Brooklyn poseurs and reverence for male auteurs, as well as a self-reflexive indicator of *Appropriate Behavior*'s distance from hipster sanctimony. Making small talk on the way to seducing him, Shirin struggles to suspend disbelief when she learns that he performs a combo stand-up/folk music act that "defies labels." He proudly proclaims, "Why does comedy always have to be so mean, at somebody's expense? I want to use my comedy to bring attention to social justice issues." Though she remains poker-faced, his piety conveys just how unsuitable a match he is for the sharp-tongued Shirin – and how preferable is Akhavan's "mean" mode of comedy. Like the post-Annie rebound date whom Alvy attempts to amuse only to have her ask, "Are you joking, or what?," Shirin's hookup is incapable of the bantering that established her connection with Maxine.

BrooklynBoy82 proves unsurprisingly vanilla as a sexual partner, so tentative (or perhaps tipsy[4]) as to be incapable of rough sex even after Shirin invites it, leaving her wistfully recalling Maxine's topping her in a flashback to happier times; the sequences are stitched together with a non-diegetic music cue: an instrumental version of Electrelane's track "Oh Sombra!," whose Spanish-language lyrics are from a sonnet by sixteenth-century Catalan poet Juan Boscán Almogávar (reprinted in translation at volume's end). Whereas Alvy resists Annie's entreaties to try smoking "grass" and likens having sex while stoned to getting "a laugh from a person who's high; it doesn't count cause they're

"*A Gay* Annie Hall" 53

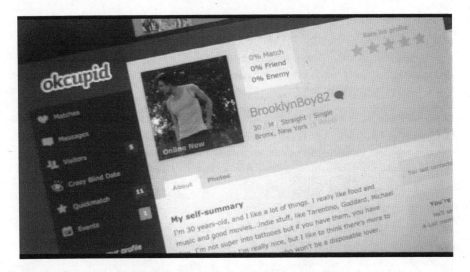

Figure 12
Trying "to forget what it felt like to be loved," Shirin cruises OKCupid and finds the anti-Maxine BrooklynBoy82, who "like[s] a lot of things."

always laughing," this romantic and erotic scene attests to Shirin and Maxine's sexual and chemical compatibility, so capable of following each other's meandering train of thought to make Maxine exclaim "We're the same kind of stoned person!" "That is so beautiful, no homo," Shirin responds, leading to the exchange discussed in act I, and then onwards:

MAXINE: I have something on my mind, but it feels too scary to say out loud.
SHIRIN: Say it.
MAXINE: Do you have anything on your mind?
SHIRIN: Maybe.
MAXINE: What?

SHIRIN: Don't be a pussy.
MAXINE: Okay, let's say it at the same time on the count of three. One ... two ...
SHIRIN: I'm falling in love with you.
MAXINE: (overlapping) I'm thinking of transitioning into a man. (*Both laugh.*) Of course, I'm falling in love with you.

Even more than during the meet-cute that culminated in their first kiss, the now-couple's "shared disregard for social norms and common human decency," as in *The Slope*, takes specific form in their (for now) mutually inappropriate language and sense of humour, as evidenced by Shirin's voicing another vulgar term for female genitalia in gently goading Maxine, whose wise-crack about gender transitioning Akhavan now finds to be (see the interview at book's end) "problematic." Yet as their shared chuckle signals, it's funny precisely because of its believability as an utterance within a lesbian couple, and so arguably is acceptable – in the way Shirin protests her right to say "dyke" – given their in-group status. As their relationship grows darker, the consensus around these matters will deteriorate.

"All Points of View"

As conflicted a fan as any #MeToo-era feminist should be about what's generally taken to be Allen's greatest work, I ultimately understand *Annie Hall* to be (and to encourage our being) critical – in a way that Allen himself certainly has not been in his real life – of its protagonist's self-aggrandizing and relationship-sabotaging impulses, and feel reassured by its resolution in uncoupling. Alvy's desire to mold Annie in his own loftily held (if also self-hating) image, pressuring her into adult education courses ("Just don't take any course where they make you read *Beowulf*") and other cerebral pursuits (Bergman

Figures 13–14
A tame tryst with BrooklynBoy82 inspires Shirin's flashback to better times with Maxine, fluidly orchestrated to Electrelane.

and Fellini films), is matched, for a time, by her eager emulation ("I think I'm starting to get more of your references"). Having disparaged Annie's "college-girl mentality" for finding Sylvia Plath's poetry "neat," Alvy presses her to read instead Ernest Becker's *The Denial of Death*. That it is Alvy who is shown here and elsewhere as excessively neurotic and controlling incrementally displaces our sympathies onto Annie, while the film unsparingly illustrates Alvy's belittling of Annie's needs (and of feminism's hard-won sexual freedoms), as in his response when she objects to his not wanting to try new things: "How can you say that? I said that you, I and that girl from your acting class should sleep together in a threesome!" The film's feminist leanings register most forcibly in Annie's growing resistance to Alvy's tutelage and worldview, as she (like us) becomes increasingly wary of, if still charmed by, somebody who admits to being "obsessed with death" and "one of the few males who suffers from [penis envy]," someone with whom "sex is a Kafkaesque experience" (that last one he doesn't deny). Annie's metamorphosis is signalled through her exchanging his reading recommendations for her own selections: first Simone de Beauvoir's feminist tract *The Second Sex*, later the conservative periodical *National Review*. "What are you turning into?" asks Alvy despairingly. "I like to try to get all points of view," she protests.

The question of whether Shirin and Maxine are good for one another is thornier, informed less by women's liberation than by tensions within LGBTQ+ politics, but stems similarly from one partner's efforts at indoctrination. In another flashback, *Appropriate Behavior* mounts its own bookstore scene, in which Maxine plies Shirin with canonical queer texts to, she says, "broaden her horizons" despite Shirin's demurral, "Oh, I don't need new reading material. I'm only up to book two of the *Twilight* series." Taking in the sober cover of *Stone Butch Blues*, Leslie Feinberg's memoir of pre-Stonewall working-class dyke life, Shirin echoes Annie's line from forty years earlier, "This is some pretty serious stuff here." "I'm asking you to read some books. You don't need to get your septum pierced – yet," is Maxine's sardonic response. Where Annie is pressured to adopt Alvy's pessimism ("I feel that life is divided into the horrible and the miserable"), Maxine's reference to sapphic septum-piercing signals her expectation that Shirin become more gay, a recollection of Akhavan's feeling of not fitting in among queerer-than-thou peers at her undergraduate alma mater Smith College, recalling, "I wasn't gay enough! I didn't have a half-shaved head and a pierced septum" (Freeman 2015).

Like Annie's retreat into *The Second Sex* or out of her own body (when Alvy denies her the "grass" she needs for sexual pleasure), sex becomes one battlefield on which Maxine grows increasingly disengaged. Attempting to spice up their "banal sex" life, she and Shirin embark on some role play with the scenario, Maxine announces that she is Shirin's tax auditor. Dubious yet game, Shirin's improvised "I've been a bad small business owner" is taken far too literally by Maxine, leading Shirin to complain, "You're killing the sexy!" Maxine gives up, calling herself "vanilla" ("Don't say that!" Shirin responds aghast) and turns away to meaningfully take up *Stone Butch Blues* from where it lay untouched by Shirin. Shirin's earlier admission to being a *Sex and the City* fan, showing her preference for the playful over the preachy, is a point on which, even while stoned, Maxine won't budge. "You've got to admit it's pretty fucking entertaining," Shirin insists. "I think it's boring," retorts Maxine. That Maxine "eschews normative feminine culture," as Catherine McDermott (2018, 91) notes, serves as a means of lesbian one-upping to undermine Shirin's credibility as queer.[5] Here as elsewhere, their disagreement traces a boundary between feminisms: on one hand a self-serious second wave, on the other a third wave willing to embrace popular feminism's commodification and sexualization, to the extent that Shirin is willing to employ her feminine wiles (however unsuccessfully) to get her needs met, even attempting to use seduction to get put on Maxine's shift at the Park Slope Food Coop. "The last time I checked, this is a cooperative," Shirin says, suggestively unbuttoning her shirt, to the disbelief of the female manager (a middle-aged hippie-type), "so why don't you cooperate with me, and I'll cooperate with you?" Undercutting

Figures 15–16
Pretty serious stuff: Attempting "to educate" their new partners, Alvy recommends *The Denial of Death* to Annie, while Maxine buys Shirin *Stone Butch Blues*.

Shirin's not terribly smooth moves, her (once again) highly inappropriate behaviour shows her putting personal whims before prohibitions against employing one's sexuality for professional gain or engaging in workplace "harassment," however drolly depicted.

Unsuccessful in that mission, Shirin feigns queer consciousness in an attempt to win back her ex. "You're not the only one who cares about gay rights," she says after crashing Maxine's reading group ("With Justice for Some"), which is focused, its facilitator announces, on "the criminal justice system and its bias against the queer community." Here again what amounts to (in legal terms) "persistent pursuit" (i.e., stalking) but is so frequently featured in romcom as to be satirized by the *Onion* under the headline "Romantic-Comedy Behavior Gets Real-Life Man Arrested" receives a sly comeuppance in this tongue-in-cheek referencing (*Onion* staff 1999). Fittingly, this social justice reading group (filmed at community coop Bluestockings) has recently displaced Dyke Knitting Circle, relocated (they're informed) to Babeland, the feminist sex boutique whose Brooklyn outpost is likely where the strap-on that Maxine unceremoniously returns to Shirin in the film's opening scene was purchased. Back at the bookstore, their bickering soon drowns out a middle-aged gay man lamenting that "consensual sex with my sixteen-year-old boyfriend" when he was eighteen has permanently branded him a sex offender, extending the film's irreverent – not to say offensive – play with such ostensibly off-limits topics as gender transitioning, sex crimes, and (as will be discussed below) religious piety.

Post-breakup, however, Maxine no longer shares Shirin's predilection for "inappropriate" humour; she goes instead to the extreme of smugly embracing the Brooklyn hipster affectations she had previously derided. Encountering one another at a party, new dates in tow, Maxine boasts that her now-girlfriend "goes to her West African dance class religiously." "Is she Black?" Shirin asks knowingly. No, naturally, yet Shirin's satisfaction in calling out this cultural appropriation is short-lived when the girlfriend turns out to be Shirin's conceited co-teacher, "former hair model" Tibet. Shirin's date, however, is the

Figures 17–18
Annie choosing *The Second Sex* over sex with Alvy; Maxine choosing *Stone Butch Blues* over role play with Shirin.

equally unsuitable kombucha-brewing, squid-inked (literally) John Francis, a poseur so "passively disinterested in everything" that Shirin finally explodes, "Seriously, what happened at Wesleyan that did this to you?" A characteristically inappropriate outburst later, and Shirin is seen sulking in the bathroom in the image that became *Appropriate Behavior*'s key art in the UK. When Maxine appears, what unfolds is not the reconciliation that conventional romcom's magical thinking might orchestrate, but rather her now-ex offering her a small measure of reassurance:

> SHIRIN: I don't know how you could try to replace me with that fetus.
> MAXINE: I'm not trying to replace you ... Take a cab home. You're gonna be okay.

In opting for the maddeningly insipid Tibet, if even just on the rebound, Maxine seems to follow Annie's post-breakup lead in embracing shallowness of the sort Shirin and Alvy renounce. With our sympathies so bound to Shirin (as they are to Alvy), we are encouraged to view Tibet as Shirin does, as having "the sex appeal of a ferret." Like Alvy, Shirin remains unreformed in her misanthropy and inappropriate behaviour, no more liable to give in to the self-righteousness embodied by Tibet – whose very name conveys her New Age-y vacuity – as Alvy is to becoming a transplanted Angeleno. In fact, on this count Shirin's sway over us is stronger even than Alvy's, whose hold often falters as we recognize things about him that he fails to see. Hearing that Tony Lacey (Paul Simon), the LA-based music producer moving in on Annie, uses the screening room of his Beverly Hills mansion nightly and even appreciates Jean Renoir's *Grand Illusion* (1937) disproves (to Annie and us) Alvy's diatribes against the supposed philistinism of Los Angeles. We get no such sense that Shirin has misjudged Tibet, who does appear (only ever viewed through Shirin's eyes) entirely insufferable.

Yet in an important swerve away from the couple dynamics in *Annie Hall*, Shirin takes after Annie in proving not so pliable to her partner's indoctrination. As signalled by their choice of reading material, it's Maxine who exhibits Alvy's anhedonia in wallowing as a means of reinforcing their respective identity groups' self-image: Alvy plays up the world-weariness of cultural Jewishness, while Maxine performs the wound-licking and past-dwelling that queer historians Heather K. Love (2010) and Nishant Shahani (2011) respectively term "feeling backward" and "reparative return." *Annie Hall*'s recurring references to ethnicity highlight the disconnect in worldviews between the privileged, racially unmarked Annie, who appears to have grown up "in a Norman Rockwell painting" and orders her pastrami on white bread with mayonnaise (provoking Alvy's eyeroll at her shiksa obliviousness), and that of midcentury American Jews whose bourgeois liberal identity was nonetheless marked as not quite white. *Appropriate Behavior* slyly signals its appropriation of *Annie Hall*'s culture clash by showing Shirin's oversexed pal Crystal flirtatiously twirling a Hasid's sidecurl, asking "How do you get them so curly?" in a callback to Alvy's visual projection of how Annie's Midwestern granny, "a classic Jew hater," views him. Like Crystal's "inappropriate" toying with cross-cultural taboos, Shirin shows similar disregard for Maxine's rainbow-flag pride, growing contemptuous of what she perceives as self-pitying, and so finding a convenient excuse for her own delayed coming out.

In both films, the coupling grows strained when the chemistry underlying their respective meet-cutes is overpowered by Jewish Alvy's and lesbian Maxine's shift into tragic registers with regard to their cultural oppression. The discrepancy between Alvy's referencing early on his Jewish alterity with dark jokes about pogroms ("My Grammy never gave gifts, she was too busy being raped by Cossacks") and his increasingly monomaniacal obsession with going to see Marcel Ophüls's four-hour documentary about French collaboration with the Nazis, *The Sorrow and the Pity* (1969), ultimately makes their cultural difference burdensome to Annie. To viewers as well, in the context of 1970s upper-middle-class Manhattan, Alvy's self-victimizing ("I distinctly heard it … Jew eat yet?") seems paranoid in a way that it would not have been in 1940s Europe or even, given anti-Semitism's alarming reemergence, today. Alvy goes

Figures 19–20
Alvy as imagined by Grammy Hall in Chippewa Falls; Crystal's brazen flirting with a Hasid outside the Park Slope Coop.

from *telling* to *being* the joke here, and so our sympathies shift ever more toward the put-upon Annie rather than the uptight Alvy, whose pal Rob admonishes "That's a very convenient out. Every time some group disagrees with you it's because of anti-Semitism."

Similar self-victimization seems at issue when Shirin expresses disbelief that her thirty-three-year-old brother Ali (Arian Moayed) is engaged, only to have her mother remind her, "I was only nineteen when I married your father." Shirin's sarcastic response ("Well, this isn't the Islamic Republic of Iran, Mom. Do you see a hijab on my head?") seems merely bratty, because the actual reality of arranged marriage – which Akhavan's own parents may well have had – seems so remote in Obama-era Brooklyn. Akhavan's experience of her ethnicity, to be explored in act III, shares important characteristics with Allen's in that their respective vantage points in post–Second World War and post-9/11 New York carry simultaneously the sense of both dislocation and discrimination; as Akhavan has stated, "I felt alienated by the Middle Eastern stories of struggle, I never quite related to them. But then the way I found myself rubbing up against the outside world I was like 'Okay, I'm different, got it'" (Erhlich, 2014). But even as Akhavan, in her *Fresh Air* interview, recalled former Iranian president Mahmoud Ahmadinejad's notorious denial of homosexuality in his nation resonating sharply with her young adult self (he made the remarks during a visit to Columbia University in 2007, around the time that Akhavan was coming out), its perverse denialism could be regarded more simply as preposterous from the relatively safe vantage point of blue-state America on the verge of *Obergefell v. Hodges*.

Long past being charmed by, and occasionally joining in with, Shirin's political incorrectness, Maxine's discontent gets voiced through virtue-signalling that increasingly grates against Shirin's dismissal of queer victimhood. Admonishing Shirin that "the only aspect of gay culture that's okay with you is drag," a fight ensues in which Maxine implicitly contrasts her own authenticity to Shirin's compromised straddling. Furiously insisting "My friends are my family. You don't know what that's like to have to choose your own family because the one you were born into –" provokes from Shirin only a snide interruption, "Enough of the lesbian orphan propaganda! We all have shit families. Of course it's a choice." Ultimately, it is Shirin's prolonged reluctance to come out to her family that most significantly undermines her and Maxine's relationship. Maxine condemns Shirin's evasions as "don't ask, don't tell," referring to the Clinton administration's widely deplored capitulation to the US military's (and electorate's) institutionalized homophobia. Accused of being "in a creepy, codependent relationship with your parents," Shirin responds, "They know, and I know they know. You think I'm a bad person because I'm not coming out on your terms." Though clearly a self-serving attempt at avoidance, we also might read this conflict as less about the importance of coming out and more about Shirin's resistance to Maxine's attempts to reshape her, and her desire to assert her own agency over the terms of her life. Fortunately sparing us the self-satisfaction ascribed to Alvy, who counts it as "a personal triumph" when he runs into Annie taking a new boyfriend to see *The Sorrow and the Pity*, *Appropriate Behavior* allows only that Shirin weighs, rather than succumbs to, Maxine's point of view. She is shown finally thumbing through *Stone Butch Blues*, yet soon enough turns to cruise OKCupid in search of BrooklynBoy82.

Queering Space and Time

Thinking back on *Annie Hall* upon the fortieth anniversary of its release, co-writer Marshall Brickman observed, "If the film is worth anything, it gives a very particular specific image of what it was like to be alive in New York at that time in that particular social-economic stratum" (Liebenson 2017). The importance of New York not only in Allen's films but for romantic comedy generally is by now a cliché, yet fittingly *Annie Hall*'s references to the city are less rose-tinted than in Allen's later work – no doubt owing to not only the city's fortunes but his own. Called by Annie "a dying city" – a line Alvy lifts

Figures 21–2
Alvy running into Annie, new partners in tow, at a screening of *The Sorrow and the Pity*; Shirin finally breaking the spine of *Stone Butch Blues*.

and inserts into his post-breakup play – derided by childhood friend Rob for its crime ("I did Shakespeare in the Park, I got mugged"), New York's decaying façade mirrors the relationship at the film's core. The city's unstoppable change – unlike "the dead shark" Alvy and Annie's relationship has become – is signalled in Rob's saying, upon returning to their old neighbourhood to show Annie the house where Alvy grew up, "You're lucky, where I used to live is now a pornographic equipment store." Though it gets a laugh for different reason now, Alvy's disbelief that Annie's "little apartment" with its "bad plumbing and bugs" rents for four hundred dollars a month foreshadows the transformation to come, in which Manhattan has been turned into a playground for the superrich. Nearly forty years later and a borough away, *Appropriate Behavior* was shot on location in a rapidly gentrifying Brooklyn, capturing a capsule of its own moment in time and place, one already disappearing into the past, as with the Kentile Floors sign visible in the film's title shot. That shot's long duration and static hold on Shirin chucking a box of her belongings collected from Maxine's apartment, dildo and strap-on harness prominently visible on top, into a dumpster only to snatch back those items before retreating, already nods at *Annie Hall*'s influence – repeating (though in reverse, and given the dildo, with a decidedly queer twist) the memorable pacing and framing that allows Alvy and Rob's ambulatory debate over anti-Semitism to unfold over an entire city block.

As these lengthy shots of surroundings that envelop their inhabitants attest, both films posit place as constitutive of oneself and one's creative work. Diehard New Yorker Alvy, in heaping derision on LA and its metonymic (for Alvy) relation to the commercial entertainment industry, with its canned laughs and endless award shows ("Greatest fascist dictator, Adolf Hitler!"), shores up *Annie Hall*'s artistic ambition in comparison, while at the same time disparaging New Yorkers' liberal elitism ("I heard that *Commentary* and *Dissent* had merged and formed *Dysentery*"). Meanwhile, *Appropriate Behavior* makes savage fun of Millennial Brooklynites' artistic pretensions: waxed Dalí mustaches, a performance artist "who's gonna dress up like a farm animal and

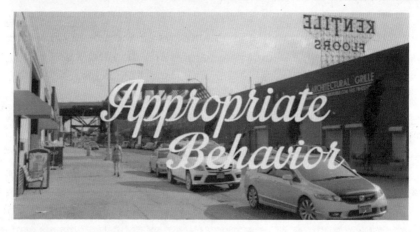

Figures 23–4
Alvy and Rob's dialogue, audible before they are visually recognizable; Shirin retreating into the distance with the former Kentile Floors sign as backdrop for *Appropriate Behavior*'s title card.

Figure 25
The dildo and harness briefly discarded.

touch herself," a roommate doing "sand castle work integrating found objects." As act II's final section contemplates further, Allen's and Akhavan's shared anti-intellectualism works as comedy specifically on the basis of its presumption that we understand its highbrow cultural referencing.

Rather than *Annie Hall*'s rosy montage of romantic spots that Alvy and Annie enjoyed as a couple to the tune of "Seems Like Old Times," *Appropriate Behavior*'s all-around less halcyon perspective resists this postcard-ready city image in favour of mapping Shirin's emotional perambulations across Brooklyn neighborhoods. From her (she admits) "too soon" co-habitation with Maxine in trendy Gowanus (where she'll attempt, and fail, in her first try to throw out the strap-on), to her despondent exile post-break-up in Bushwick ("This is not a home. This is a refugee camp," brother Ali tells her; "You don't know what 'cool Brooklyn loft' looks like," she retorts unconvincingly), to her delinquent standing at the lesbian-certified Park Slope Food Coop, where (Crystal reminds her) "no amount of wholesale spelt sushi was worth the emotional toll" of the shifts required of its members – the nomadic trajectory marks Shirin's in-betweener movements among, never quite settling into, these spaces. Where her love/hate ambivalence around the (self-described) coolest borough speaks to Shirin's conflicted feelings about love and life, Alvy's unrelenting contempt for LA mirrors his own rigid, self-sure ways.

The clearest evidence of its debt to, and reworking of, *Annie Hall*, the flashbacks that subsume us within heartsick Shirin's memories visually conjure the experience of nostalgia and loss, but go further to resist, in their circularity and open-endedness, the twin teleological drives of queer romantic comedy and of homonormativity generally: coming out and couple (re)formation. Though now a recognized milestone on the map of an LGBTQ+ person's life, it bears remembering that the modern invention of coming out (and its related conception of the closet) was a liberation-era tool for personal and political action. Yet as queer theorists Eve Kosofsky Sedgwick (2008 [1990]) and Judith Butler (1999 [1990]) caution, to come out is to position oneself against one repressive regime (homophobia) by taking up one's place in another (heteronormativity) – and, by virtue of coming out's own eventual normalization, still another (homonormativity). In this view, the ritualized confessional act (which the coming-out narrative of countless queer films works to inculcate) masks these power relations and operations with a promise of personal authenticity and liberation that belies actual social and political conditions. It is this illusory path towards fulfillment and finitude that *The Slope* slyly challenged with its "It Gets Better?" parody, and that *Appropriate Behavior* bypasses in leaving Shirin's coming out unresolved.

Shirin's "failure" to come out on Maxine's terms will be examined in act III in its entanglement with Shirin's in-betweener identity positions as bisexual and Persian. Here we see *Appropriate Behavior*'s nonlinear structure further exceeding its antecedent's purpose (to narrate *Annie Hall*'s story according to Alvy's self-serving recollection); it functions as a resistant force, or temporal drag, against culturally prescribed forms of "growth." Queer theory's defamiliarization of time itself as a social construct reveals the elevation of linearity, continuity, progress, and futurity as structural concepts deployed towards the reproduction of privilege. Elizabeth Freeman terms *chrononormativity* the institutionally and ideologically enforced schedules by which social subjects are regulated for maximum conformity and productivity. Together with what Dana Luciano (following Hannah Arendt and Michel Foucault) terms the *chronobiopolitical* forces that shape "'the sexual arrangement of the time of life' of entire populations," this imposed timeline defines normative subjects – what Freeman refers to as "properly temporalized bodies" – and operates through the validation of temporal markers, or milestones, that map appropriate (read: conformist and productive) lifestyles (Freeman 2010, 3–4). Where straight culture's fetishization of biological procreation constructs menstruation, virginity, marriage, childbirth, and menopause as key markers, the reorientation for queer timelines gives arguably greatest emphasis to coming out.

Whitney Monaghan points to (white cis-het) male reviewers' criticisms of *Appropriate Behavior*'s nonlinearity (something *Annie Hall* was hardly criticized for) and insightfully formulates its significance as both in-betweener and queer: "By positioning Shirin as a figure caught between these two identities, Akhavan uses the question of 'appropriateness' to challenge the temporality associated with teleological and progressive/progressing milestones. Akhavan's film suggests that it is not enough to substitute heteronormative milestones with 'queer' ones. Rather, it suggests that we must critique the politics of value underpinning the supposed necessity of attaining these milestones" (2016, 156). As Monaghan notes, Shirin's recombination and revaluation of straight and queer milestones enable her in-betweener navigation of and deviation from heteronormative and homonormative life paths. It bears recalling here Claire Perkins's observation, quoted in act I, that Akhavan's work critiques these timelines, with her onscreen selves embodying "emotional awkwardness ... to reframe the question of what counts as 'productive' to what counts as 'appropriate,' and in doing so illuminates a range of 'alternate forms of living'" (2016, 150).

Fittingly, in *Appropriate Behavior*'s final scene, Shirin and Crystal voice disbelief at the "appropriate" timeline dictated by (neo)traditional romcom, with its entreaties to women to remain sexually chaste until marriage – or at least until after a few dates. Having expressed interest in having a threesome of her own (with Shirin's goth roommates), Crystal muses, "There are people in this world who go on dates that are perfectly great, and then they wait awhile before they engage in sexual contact." "That's disgusting," Shirin responds, deadpan. "I'm pretty sure it happens outside New York," says Crystal, agreeing. As the film's final words of dialogue, their ironic mockery of the sexually conservative logic that condemns "promiscuity" as practised by "urban elites" as "disgusting" harkens back to Alvy's own assessment of his chosen tribe: "The rest of the country looks upon New York like we're left-wing Communist, Jewish, homosexual pornographers. I think about us that way sometimes, and I live here." Rejecting the assimilationist coupling of so many gay romantic comedies and the homonormative culture that produces them, *Appropriate Behavior* presents as the film's final coupling (platonic) girlfriends who identify as bi (Shirin) and heteroflexible (Crystal), but whose mutual logic of desire is decidedly queer. The Rhoda to Shirin's Mary, the Ilana to her Abbi, Crystal's even greater penchant for inappropriate behaviour – flirting with the Hasid, talking about having the hots for Shirin's father, confessing to carnal knowledge of perpetually stoned dad Ken ("He's that investment banker in my parents' building I used to hook up with in high school") – Crystal queers the "straight friend" character in a way that twists the fair-haired girl-next-door archetype and affirms the erstwhile stigma of immoderate, "depraved" sexual appetites typically affixed to queers.[6]

One further revisionist twist on romcom's conventional couple formation follows, as the camera angle narrows to isolate Shirin in the frame, holding on her as the diegetic sound gives way to a musical track that continues to play over the end credits. By virtue of its framing and duration, this final shot knowingly alludes to the iconic last image of *The Graduate*, in which the runaway couple rides off into an indeterminate sunset to the strains of Simon and Garfunkel's "The Sound of Silence." The lyrics to Electrelane's "To the East," the track that comes in over *Appropriate Behavior*'s final shot and continues through the end credits, explicitly comment on the diegetic action at this moment, when Shirin catches sight of Maxine waiting on the East Ninth Street subway platform. The two meet eyes for a startled moment before Maxine raises a hand in acknowledgment. A beat later, just before the train departs, Shirin does the same. The film's last spoken words, the automated warning "Stand clear of the closing doors, please," sounds a note of finality as a slight smile comes across Shirin's face and the song, with its title's gesture at movement and dawn, builds in volume to drown out all else. Yet as the lyrics commence, any confidence that emotional closure or narrative resolution have been reached is undermined by their plaintive, repeated pining, "Come back to me." This second use of Electrelane – an all-female act of the 2000s with a fervent fanbase of queer women – links us back to the band's "Oh Sombra!" that appeared non-diegetically in the love scene between Shirin and Maxine, thus continuing the wistful looping back in time.[7]

Here again *Appropriate Behavior* borrows only to progress from its forebear, insofar as, for all *The Graduate*'s "radical romcom" status, in having its (straight, white, Hollywood-beautiful) heroine abandon the man she's just married in favour of her mother's ex-lover, it's a decidedly pre-feminist film, and film ending. Nearly fifty years on, *Appropriate Behavior* renews this iconic final image's radical force by presenting, instead of a straight white couple, an uncoupled queer woman of colour. As a coming-out narrative, as well, this ending is purposefully, and radically, both inclusive and inconclusive; to conclude with a single and (still) bisexual Shirin travelling to her own uncertain future circles back to the film's start, when she was crying en route to her (now-former) home to collect her things and not nearly out of the tunnel, so

Figure 26
Shirin, post-breakup, at film's start.

to speak. Derailing the coming-out teleology, *Appropriate Behavior*'s open-ended circularity suits queer conceptions of sexual selfhood as constantly in flux, as becoming rather than being. While debunking the (neo)traditional tropes of sunsets-and-soulmates and the LGBTQ+ romcom's coming-out-and-coupling, this ending reconnects to the radical romcoms of the women's liberation era in showing Shirin having finally become "a woman in charge of her sexuality and not afraid of change."

Farts over Art

One last look back at *Annie Hall* reveals another important element it shares with *Appropriate Behavior*, their self-reflective referencing of their own processes of artistic creation. Much as Alvy Singer's turning forty impels him to

Figures 27–8
Iconic, indeterminate final shots: *The Graduate* and *Appropriate Behavior*.

reflect on lost love Annie ("I still can't get my mind around that"), Allen himself hit forty, and Akhavan reached thirty, around the time their respective films were released. At these pivotal stages of life, both filmmakers brought to their autobiographical works an inclination to reflect on one's art as a means of self-inscription – both informed by and formative of one's selfhood – yet the formal strategies each adopts reflects a divergence in the degree of creative licence each artist affords themselves. Akhavan's borrowing of *Annie Hall*'s nonlinear narrative structure signals her debt to that film – one that is, as they say, made in the editing – yet devises a different internal logic for ordering scenes. Rather than *Annie Hall*'s deferring to Alvy's expository voiceover to direct our path through the story, *Appropriate Behavior* uses the equally seamless "match cut" to steer us across scenes that flashback in time.

Such cutting together of two shots with a consistent visual (or aural) element permits places, objects, or phrases to act as Proustian madeleines for triggering memory, as in the shot of Shirin forlornly looking into a bar that carries us back to the night she and Maxine spent celebrating Pride there. Earlier in the film, a more complex flashback transition uses as its cue a phrase of dialogue that jumps not only across time and space, but across films. Reassuring Shirin that she was right to end it with Maxine, Crystal's reminder that "She wasn't even fucking you towards the end" prompts Shirin's weak protest, "Maybe it was a phase." On first viewing and at this early moment in *Appropriate Behavior* the phrase's import is not clear. Crystal's referencing here of Shirin's unsatisfying sex life with Maxine, coupled with the earlier scene's showing Shirin retrieving the strap-on that reappears, in a sly sight-gag, ready for action on the then couple's bedside table, makes for a fluid transition into flashback. Yet because there is no precise visual bridge between these shots (as there is in the Pride bar transition), another aural trigger could be said to emanate from an extradiegetic scene: that in which Annie, avoiding sex with Alvy, says "It's just that I'm going through a phase, that's all." Given the role play attempt abandoned after Maxine's mood-killing that follows,

Figure 29
The dildo that goes unused making an appearance in the first flashback.

Shirin and we are surely justified in suspecting Maxine's motives in devising a scenario so unsexy as to involve paperwork – clearly a sign that sex for them had become a matter of box-checking.

Still another instance is the previously discussed transition in which Shirin's disappointing hook-up leads her to recall the passionate sex – and declarations of love – previously shared with Maxine. Like Alvy's imagining that every passerby is as preoccupied as he by his romantic travails, *Appropriate Behavior*'s seamless segues meld present and past as a means to subsume us within Shirin's heartsick wallowing. Yet this memory-driven design constitutes an important departure from *Annie Hall*'s use of editing to conjure wish-fulfilling illusions, whether of having Marshall McLuhan himself step in to prove a point or envisioning his childhood classmates as adults. Alvy's voiceover cops to his having "some trouble [distinguishing] between fantasy and reality," yet as this selective memory turns towards his relationship with Annie, it becomes increasingly self-serving – as in travelling back to see Annie's exes, treated to Alvy's ridicule so as to suggest he is the better choice, and ultimately going so far as to quite literally caricature (through animation) Annie as the Evil Queen. In contrast, fantasy in *Appropriate Behavior* is heard, not seen, as in utterances like Shirin's wishfully thinking of herself and Maxine as "an It Couple." "Not really," demurs Crystal. What we see of Shirin's past with Maxine, however selectively remembered, is bounded by reality – unlike Alvy's surreal fantasies, concocted wholly to serve his self-interest. As he admits, "You're always trying to get things to come out perfect in art because it's real difficult in life." *Annie Hall* works (still to my mind) so brilliantly because Alvy's self-aggrandizing and self-deprecating impulses go hand in hand; he's an unreliable yet irresistible narrator, chiefly on account of his, and the film's, killing wit. In contrast, Alvy's self-indulgent attempt to turn his life into "Art" with a play based on his relationship with Annie fails for being humourless and poorly performed, despite following (from what we hear) an identical script.

Though Akhavan grasps that the creative potential to be mined from solipsism functions best at an ironic remove, Shirin (like Akhavan's other alter egos) is no less snarky for remaining more reliably rooted in reality. Akhavan distinguishes her film from *Annie Hall*, and amplifies her own distinctive voice as an emerging filmmaker, by the secondary storyline based on Akhavan's former job at an organization called Video Kid Brooklyn. Believing it will be an easy gig with teenage Park Slope overachievers, Shirin forgoes lesson planning ("What is this, Germany? I could lock them in a room with a half-eaten apple and a Tic-Tac and come back to the Mona Lisa"). Shirin's surprise and chagrin at having to herd a crew of hyperactive six-year-old boys, "roughly a decade younger that I was expecting," has her attempt to resign, but persuaded by hapless boss Ken ("It's just fake it 'til you make it"), she sticks with it. Undercut by fellow teacher Tibet, under whose tutelage the advanced class (composed entirely of girls) is orchestrating a shot-by-shot remake of a scene from Hitchcock's *The Birds* (1963), Shirin struggles to control her hyperactive brood. Unable to get them to sit still for the duration of the minute-long 1896 film *The Kiss*, during which one boy protests "That's not 'propriate for our age!," Shirin finally gives in to their collective vision: "To make a movie about farts!" At the screening that concludes Shirin's teaching stint, after the advanced class's virtuously multicultural montage filmed in "artful" black and white complete with chess-playing twins (which I read as Akhavan's wink at *The Seventh Seal* [1957] and *The Shining* [1980]), the "not-advanced class" unfurls their flatulent opus *The Lost Fart*. The instinct that inspires Shirin's charges, juxtaposed with the auteur-worshipping imitativeness of Tibet's didactic approach, ultimately yields the more original and authentic-feeling work, one that we as viewers laugh complicitly with rather than knowingly at, one that (as Shirin protested of another guilty pleasure) "you've got to admit [is] pretty fucking entertaining."

Much as *Annie Hall* endorses its own tone, by turns funny and melancholy, over and above the mawkish amateur theatrics of Alvy's play-within-a-film, *Appropriate Behavior* embraces the lighthearted irreverence of lowbrow comedy over the pompously self-important art film in having Shirin and Ken agree, "Farts *are* funny." It's an apt review, given its filmmaker's fondness for describing *Appropriate Behavior* as "forty per cent fart jokes." Of course, the joke's on those who mistake either it or *Annie Hall* for actually being lowbrow. Both employ what social critic Pierre Bourdieu (1986 [1979]) terms "high culture comedy" in their reliance on cognitive cues, cultural referencing, and contemplative affect designed to play to those with the educational capital and cultural sophistication to appreciate its humour. *Annie Hall*'s in-jokes privilege urban sophisticates and specifically the Jewish New York liberal intellectual that Alvy, like Allen, embodies (see Symons 2013, 118–27). At the same time, NYU dropout Allen proclaims his regular-guy status by Alvy's mockery of a blowhard academic's pontificating, overheard in a movie theater lobby, and by his sneaking away from a party of literati to watch a Knicks game. Similarly, for all Akhavan's appreciative nods to "artistes" like Breillat, Cholodenko, and the first generation of Mumblecore filmmakers, she readily

Figures 30–1
Trying to teach kids to appreciate film history by screening *The Kiss*; the all-girl advanced class's emulating of Bergman and Kubrick.

confesses to having retained her earliest tastes, which were hardly highbrow, recalling, "It wasn't like my parents were cinephiles; they were immigrants who watched shows like *Two and a Half Men* [2003–15]" (Wickham 2015).[8] The significance of her family's influence and that of their cultural heritage, both for *Appropriate Behavior* and on Akhavan's own bisexuality, are the focus of act III.

Act III
"An Iranian Bisexual Teacher"

I see a real parallel between being bisexual and being the child of immigrants. I don't feel American, and I don't feel Iranian. And yet, I feel very much both and neither at the same time ... You live in the gray area. You're somewhere in between. It's a very uncomfortable place to be. But it's home, so I'll take it.

Desiree Akhavan on *Fresh Air*

"Living in the Gray Area"

Prompted by Akhavan's reflection above, this third and final act ponders the parallel Akhavan draws between her sexuality and her ethnicity. Having previously applied the term *in-betweener* to Akhavan's sexual, cultural, and professional positioning, I take my cue from her description of these "parallel" aspects of her experience and selfhood as I explore how they have shaped her creative work and its significance for her audience. These parallel lines, which serve as the chief source of the protagonists' narrative conflict in *Appropriate Behavior* and *The Bisexual*, are tricky, often impossible, to separate.[1] In both works, the inevitable entanglement of these two deep-seated facets of Akhavan's identity makes for profound creative material to mine. At the same time, these are hardly the sole defining aspects of Akhavan's selfhood. For all the centrality of bisexuality in her body of work, Akhavan is quick to note, "So much of my life has nothing to do with being bisexual" (Kachka 2015). Nonetheless, her bisexuality was omnipresent in the press coverage around *Appropriate Behavior*, so much so that it inspired her 2018 television series, discussed in the finale that follows. In a similar spirit, Akhavan reports having had a decidedly "normal" American upbringing: "I was raised on the same bullshit television as everyone else, I grew up on 'The Brady Bunch,' being bisexual or Iranian didn't change that" (Ehrlich 2014).

As with the other press-favoured moniker as "the next Lena Dunham," here again Akhavan beat them to the punch, having playfully noted of her peer, in her "Who Wrote It Better?" piece, "Thank god she's not Iranian or bisexual." So too does Shirin introduce herself as "an Iranian bisexual teacher" to the LGBTQ+ reading group, just before brazenly asking out its discussion facilitator, alluring law professor Sasha, in a bid to make Maxine jealous. As with Anh Duong in the role of Shirin's mother, this comprises another instance of inspired casting for having Aimee Mullins – she of the Paralympics, Alexander McQueen runway, TED Talks, Cremaster films (1996–2005), and *Stranger Things* (2016–)[2] – be the consummate catch, and so making Shirin look irresistible, if only to herself, when Sasha concedes to the date. "I couldn't have refused even if I wanted to. All those people," she'll later chide Shirin, who responds mortifyingly, "I will invite them all to our wedding." Intending to show up Maxine (who leaves in a huff) while also proving her social-justice-mindedness, Shirin's half-forthright, half-fatuous self-identification in this moment displays her taking to heart Ken's advice to "fake it 'til you make it." One of Shirin's brash shows of overconfidence – as with her informing Maxine at their first meeting, "I'm super sexy and I'm super into girls" – this too gets results, at least in the moment.

Akhavan explains having shaped this aspect of Shirin's character in direct defiance of representational norms: "I wanted to make Shirin real and entitled.

Figure 32
Sasha (Aimee Mullins) as the dream date designated to make Shirin's ex jealous.

Whenever I see people from marginalised communities depicted in films – be they gay, Middle Eastern or whatever – they're treated as either noble or a joke. Or in the case of Iranians, they're treated as villains. I really wanted to make Shirin a multi-dimensional character that you can relate to on a lot of levels" (Levine 2015). This entitlement in the face of disenfranchisement is another element of the in-betweener position that she and her screen selves resolutely occupy. On the one hand, being first-world, educated, financially secure, and cisgender, they are patently advantaged; on the other, they are judged as immaturely and inauthentically clinging to a sexuality stopgap – as the saying goes, "bi now, gay later." Moreover, they are women in a heteropatriarchal industry and culture, *and* are (in Sharmila Sen's formulation [2018]) "not quite white" in a post-9/11 climate of escalating Islamophobia and white supremacy. Possessing some measure of privilege and cultural capital, and thus security and recognition, while at the same time having the experience of nonbelonging as a result of feeling unsafe, alone, and unseen – this is clearly an experience that speaks to many beyond those identifying as bisexual or living in the Iranian diaspora. No doubt this is a key reason that Akhavan's work resonates powerfully with many viewers.

Like Shirin's excess confidence, Akhavan's defiant "oversharing" – as some would term her entitled insistence on speaking her mind – is clearly key to the persona she cultivates onscreen and off, and links her all the more to Lena Dunham, whose own brand of oversharing has been both celebrated and deplored. This outspokenness is born of Akhavan's experience of being made to feel silenced and compelled to compartmentalize as a closeted young adult, as she recalls: "I don't ever want to feel ashamed, or to feel like I'm keeping secrets. Like when I was 19 I had my first heartbreak. It was with a woman and I was a mess, and I couldn't tell my parents about it. I felt so lost, and I ended up feeling pressured into getting a nose job, which is like this Persian rite of passage, and most Iranian girls I meet have had one" (Wickham 2015). A blatant case of the clash between sexuality and cultural tradition that continues to inform her work, Akhavan drew on the experience for creative inspiration: her NYU graduate thesis film *Nose Job*, a nine-minute short about an awkward Persian teen whose friend pays her the decidedly left-handed compliment, "Your mom is so beautiful. You look more like your dad though." The logline: "Nothing says I love you like rhinoplasty." While the initial conception of *Appropriate Behavior* contained little that dealt with her Persian heritage, at producer Cecilia Frugiuele's urging Akhavan rewrote the script to include scenes drawn from her family. In its final realization, *Appropriate Behavior* goes even further, to suggest that cultural heritage and family ties are not easily extricated from the process of identifying and coming to terms with one's sexuality.

In contrast with what I'll describe below as bisexuality's invisibility, Akhavan's non-Anglo-Saxon origins are signalled through her name and appearance, to a degree she satirizes in Shirin's job interview with Ken, who first greets her as "Ginny," then after being corrected inquires excitedly, "What is that? Libyan, Armenian, Argentinian?" On hearing she's Iranian, he enthuses about a recent *Vice* read on Tehran's underground hip-hop scene, asking hopefully, "So you're part of that?" Shirin's response, that her yearly trips there are spent "watching Disney videos with my grandmother while she untangles jewelry," clearly disappoints Ken, who will go on to get her name wrong on every meeting until, finally, upon congratulating her on *The Lost Fart*, he manages to address her correctly. Yet the film's treatment of his microaggressions remains lighthearted, Ken being a lovable yet feckless character. In an earlier jab at workplace tokenism, Shirin explains quitting her job at the *Brooklyn Paper* by way of saying, "The only reason they hired me in the first place is 'cos they wanted a Middle Eastern person. Now that Yavah's in Editorial, everyone's gushing over how Syrian she is." As she does so casually here, Shirin's referencing of her ethnicity as a convenient means for rationalizing her choices will be the cause of the deepening rift in her relationship with Maxine, as prefigured when the couple travels to New Jersey for a party celebrating Nowruz, the Persian New Year.

"Liberace's Wet Dream"

Conceding to come as Shirin's "white friend" rather than her date, Maxine warns Shirin against repeatedly "playing the Persian card" to justify not coming out to her family. Shirin responds indignantly, "I'm sorry, what country is it that you get stoned to death if you're convicted of being gay? Oh, yeah. Wait, I know. It's Iran. The country that my entire family comes from!" Yet we'll come to see, upon meeting Shirin's family, that this remark is mostly self-serving, since Shirin's parents' age and secularism identify them as being among the generation of Persians to have left Iran precisely because of the postrevolutionary theocracy whose persecutions Shirin references. Hence their status as (in Shirin's words) "half-assed Iranians" who compromise their traditions, on Nowruz and otherwise, in service to their Americanized ways.

But while not traditionalist guardians of either culture's strictures, Shirin's parents are ethnically and generationally disposed to conservative thinking and values, and in their first appearance voice belittling flattery and barbed humour that implicitly maintain gendered norms. Mother Nasrin shows off to her son's fiancée Shirin's "stunning" hands and encourages her to go into hand modelling, while father Mehrdad (Hooman Majd) jokes that his urologist son "loves the penises so much" and professes relief that Shirin is boyfriend-less so "thank god I don't have to get my shotgun ready." "Good one, Dad," Shirin says sarcastically. Not even at film's end are we sure how fully Shirin uses the threat of familial disapproval, even disowning, as a crutch – given the disregard with which her mother greets Shirin coming out, discussed below. Yet as the often-reported experience of both queer youth and children of immigrants attests, such concerns about disappointing or humiliating one's parents are deeply felt if not always well-founded. As Akhavan observes, "I think all of us are motivated by wanting to do well by our parents – that's like the universal truth, but especially so for the children of immigrants" (Freeman 2015). It's clear from testimonials bearing titles like "You're My Only Hope: A Love Letter to Desiree Akhavan," published on the Girls on Tops site upon their launch of the Akhavan-branded shirt, that *Appropriate Behavior* offers Middle Eastern queer women, much as it does bisexuals, a feeling of compassionate comradeship (Tatevosian 2014). As Akhavan related on *Fresh Air* about the Persian community she grew up within, "You don't talk about ugly things … you just turn your head the other way. So I didn't even hear of one Iranian homosexual my whole life. And when I came out, it was like coming out as a leprechaun or a unicorn. It was like a fictitious thing" (Akhavan and Danforth 2018). These considerable powers of denial are on display at the Nowruz gathering Maxine attends despite her concern about "being in enclosed spaces where I can't detect any visibly gay people." Shirin attempts to reassure her by sharing the suspicion that "Uncle Neema's harboring some bi-curious tendencies," but asked whether they have talked about it, Shirin replies, "Of course not. Persians communicate mostly through gossip." This avoidance of self-revelation is then exemplified in Shirin's exchange with a clique of "ideal Persian daughters" (recalling *Appropriate Behavior*'s logline). Briefly engaging the undercover couple in conversation consisting of swapping self-deprecating barbs (prompting Shirin's "Before model for Accutane" self-putdown), they abruptly make a beeline for another guest after Shirin ventures an emotionally honest remark. "What just happened?" Maxine says confusedly, leaving Shirin to explain how their encounters follow an identical script every Nowruz.

So precariously bordering on queer is the party pageantry that, upon entering, Maxine sums it up as "like we just stepped into Liberace's wet dream." "Isn't it spectacular?" agrees Shirin. Fittingly, this assessment hints at the community's ostensible insistence on staying closeted, predicting what some time later Maxine will refer to as a "don't ask, don't tell" protocol. The sequence's shot–reverse shot structure allows Shirin and Maxine a frame of their own so long as they appear platonic and gender-conforming (Maxine having been instructed to wear a dress). The rules of decorum even permit same-sex dancing, during which Akhavan permits the camera to move freely as well. Yet in the earlier exchange with the clique of Shirin's peers, the shot composition cordons off "appropriate" from "inappropriate" female groupings to visually set Shirin apart, underlining her failure to assimilate among her hyperfeminine, presumably straight peers.

This pattern of shot composition characterizes those scenes that convey Shirin's ill-fitting presence within her Persian community and family, also seen in her trip home for *chai*, the traditional Persian tea ritual that often serves as an opportunity for parents to vet their offspring's marriage prospects. Single and not out to her family, Shirin is crowded into what seems as if it ought to be a two-shot alongside mother Nasrin and father Mehrdad, visually embodying what Maxine will harshly if not inaccurately characterize as "a creepy codependent relationship with your parents" (the creepiness is intensified when we recall the other scene in which Shirin shares a sofa with a

Figures 33–4
Shirin with "white friend" Maxine, set apart from the "ideal Persian daughters" with whom she "communicates mostly through gossip" and self-deprecating flattery.

couple, the swingers who pick her up in a bar). Clinching this positioning of Shirin as childlike and underachieving, sitting opposite them in their own two-shot are "good Persian son" Ali and his fiancée Layli. Not just high-achieving surgeons, each is directly engaged in saving children, Ali as a pediatric urologist (also Akhavan's real-life brother's profession) and Layli through reconstructive plastic surgery – not, as Shirin needles her, for "middle-aged housewives with low self-esteem" but, Ali smugly interjects, for kids needing burn treatment and skin grafting. "Cool," Shirin says, chastened.

Uncoupled, unemployed, and unladylike, Shirin as embodiment of failure to personify the ideal Persian daughter is conveyed narratively and visually. Fittingly, the familial discussion in this scene reprimands not just Shirin's singledom but her having (in Ali's words) "done jack shit with your degree." Her "improperly temporalized body" (recalling Elizabeth Freeman's formulation) is situated in spatial terms at a remove from and in opposition to her successful brother and future sister-in-law's professional and romantic maturity. Not only are the latter two's engagement (and presumed future procreation) in accord with socially approved life scripts, by virtue of their professions they are actively invested in ensuring the child=future equivalency central to Western neoliberal capitalism – the ideology that queer theory names *reproductive futurism* (Edelman 2004). In questioning this conflation of procreation with capitalist preservation and productivity, queer theory reappropriates the notion of queerness as failure, which (Karl Schoonover finds) "often looks a lot like wasted time, wasted lives, wasted productivity," so as to affirm it as a route to anti-capitalist resistance and queer world-building (2012, 73).

Clearly still caught within, but chafing against, her familial-cultural perception of (albeit unspoken) queer failure, Shirin meanwhile acquires an inverse stigma as failed queer in Maxine's eyes. Taking in Maxine's fascination with the (as she says) "beautiful ritual" of jumping over fire at Nowruz, Shirin teases her by saying, "Ew, you are totally having one of those 'I'm dating an immigrant' moments, like 'Isn't learning about other cultures so fun and enriching!'" Yet as will emerge, Maxine's enthusiastic acceptance of

Figures 35–6
Sharing *chai* with her family, single and closeted Shirin is consigned as childlike, separate from and in opposition to her successful sibling and future sister-in-law.

Shirin's ethnicity stems from it posing no threat to Maxine's whiteness, whereas Shirin's closeted bisexuality troubles Maxine's lesbian self-perception and politics.

Much as Electrelane's "Oh Sombra!" conjures up Shirin's reminiscence of her and Maxine's lustful past, Middle Eastern pop music provides an aural bridge from the flashback to the Nowruz celebration Maxine attends, forward to the present-day lovesick Shirin finally (if briefly) attempting to read *Stone Butch Blues*. The song's fusing of the film's past and present temporalities and their queer-suppressing and queer-embracing spaces (New Jersey and a Bushwick loft respectively) suggest that Shirin's compartmentalizing of these conflicting worlds has come to seem to her untenable and undesirable. Yet the recognition comes too late and is not yet backed up by action. It will take Shirin until the third act, and the next Nowruz, to come out to her family – fitting given that the American New Year commenced Shirin and Maxine's coupling, and the first Nowruz gave Shirin cover for bringing together – without fully commingling – her two lives. Using this pattern of repetition with a difference that Catherine McDermott names "asymmetric reciprocity" (2018, 103), the initial dialogue from the meet-cute, which has Maxine find Shirin outside on the stoop, is echoed at the second Nowruz when Ali, also finding Shirin alone outside the party, repeats the question. "What are you doing out here?" "Social anxiety," her answer to Maxine, is rephrased meaningfully in her response to her brother: "Hiding."

Our awareness that this loaded word, uttered on the cusp of Shirin's coming out, would have far graver implications were her family living under theocratic rule in Iran (rather than "half-assed Iranians" partying in New Jersey) prompts a brief detour to consider a final dimension of *Appropriate Behavior*'s cinematic lineage. Akhavan's corpus clearly belongs within, and benefits from consideration as, what postcolonial theorist Hamid Naficy (himself Iranian American) calls "accented cinema" (2001), those works thematizing the experience of exile and diaspora. Though the Iranian New Wave of the 1960s put the pre-revolutionary nation's filmmaking on the international map, in the wake of the 1979 Islamic-led authoritarian regime's takeover and in the forty-plus years since, Iranian filmmakers who remained in the homeland have persevered against formidable odds. Two-time Academy Award–winning director Asghar Farhadi (*A Separation*, 2011; *The Salesman*, 2016) was prevented from attending the Oscars ceremony in 2017 as a result of the Trump administration's travel ban on Muslim-majority nations, while Jafar Panahi has secretly made and smuggled into distribution multiple films while sitting out regime-ordered house arrest in Tehran. Akhavan has spoken of the significance that artist-novelist-filmmaker Marjane Satrapi's *Persepolis* (2007) has for her, and Satrapi and other Iranian-born women filmmakers – notably two generations of Makhmalbafs (Marzieh, stepmother to siblings Samira and Hana), as well as France-based actor Golshifteh Farahani and visual artist Shirin Neshat – have gained global acclaim for work whose first-hand experience complicates and resists what Patricia White describes as the dominant representations of Iran in the west: "parables of oppression and liberation, dramas of veiling and unveiling" in the context of a censorious regime (2015, 90). On the heels of those artists' Third Way/ve feminist intervention, Akhavan and her second-generation Iranian American cohort – which includes Maryam Keshavarz (*Circumstance*, 2011) and Ana Lily Amirpour (*A Girl Walks Home Alone at Night*, 2014), have added another layer of complexity and irreverence in voicing queer women's experience within the diaspora.

Circumstance calls particularly to be put in dialogue with *Appropriate Behavior*, as it was also made by a New York–born and raised Iranian American and centres on two young women's illicit love, all the more illicit for being set in present-day Tehran (though filmed in Beirut, Lebanon). Melodramatic where *Appropriate Behavior* skews comedic, the films nevertheless share an implicit kinship shown most keenly through their uncannily similar final shots. Again the repetition with a difference speaks volumes: where Shirin heads single but hopeful into the New York cityscape, *Circumstance*'s final shot shows tearful and veiled teenager Ati (Nikohl Boosheri) travelling alone to an uncertain future in Dubai, having been sent away by her wealthy parents to prevent her endangering best friend Shireen's (Sarah Kazemy) arranged marriage to Ati's radicalized brother, an informant for the Morality Police. Where Akhavan's Shirin controls the film's narration through the memory-driven nonlinear structure, the recurring motif of surveillance imagery in *Circumstance* indicates the panoptical gaze that watches women's nearly every move under a totalitarian patriarchal regime. As both this closing image and pervasive visual patterning illustrate, and as the name they share (though with slightly changed transliteration) makes all too resonant, Shirin's fate could have been drastically altered had her family history been only marginally different.

"The Last Taboo"

Although raised in suburban New York at a far remove from the theocratic regime, Akhavan has made frequent reference to the painful process of coming out to her family, recalling, "None of us had ever met an Iranian gay person that we knew of. It was unspoken completely, so we were all in shock and nobody knew what the future would look like for me" (Kermode 2015). Their year-long estrangement and only gradual reconciliation leads Akhavan to believe she would have avoided it if possible: "If I were hot in high school, if a man had seduced me, I never would have come out. I wouldn't have allowed myself to fall in love with a woman, because it was such a horror to my family" (Stanford 2018). To compound the already challenging issue, she was coming out as bisexual.

Bisexuality is, as a review of Akhavan's brazenly titled 2018 series *The Bisexual* asserted, "the last taboo" (SBS Staff 2019). So too is it, unlike virtually all other identity formations, still ripe for mockery; as Andrew Rannells's character Elijah on *Girls* memorably quipped, "Bisexuals are like the last group you can make fun of. Bisexuals and Germans." That both assessments about bisexuality are all too true, Akhavan knows well – and as fans of *The Slope*

Figure 37
Circumstance's final shot, uncannily similar to but a world apart from that of *Appropriate Behavior*.

can attest, she is not above a bit of self-mockery in performing, as her exaggerated onscreen self, what she admits to being "the worst aspects of my sexuality" (Akhavan and White 2015).

As indicated by act II's discussion of queer temporalities and *Appropriate Behavior*'s unresolved, cyclical-not-linear coming out (circled back to below), bisexuals are hardly alone among queer folx in having to blaze uncharted lifepaths and establish alternative milestones, or in experiencing coming out as something one does not once but consistently and repeatedly. Yet bisexuality is distinctively disadvantaged, in both personal and representational terms, by what I call in my book *The B Word: Bisexuality in Contemporary Film and Television* (2013) its *(in)visibility*: the simultaneous presence and absence that issue from its deniability and illegibility. Its resilience nonetheless attests, in both our cultural lexicon and representational landscape, to its salience and also its adaptability.

Akhavan's distinctive way of depicting bisexuality unfolds within a context in which not just bisexuality's representation but its very raison d'être is regularly called into question. Whereas the cultural presumption of heterosexuality gives way in certain spaces (a gay bar, for instance) to a presumption of homosexuality, in virtually no situations or contexts are people presumed bisexual. A related commonality of bisexual experience stems from the hiding-in-plain-sight sense encapsulated by Akhavan's observation that "It's the one sexuality where you're defined by whoever your partner is at that moment" (Davidson 2015), an absurd notion not least for being directed at an identity which presupposes *de*prioritization of gendered object choice.

Veering from the unknown quantity that queerness constituted for her Persian family, a different form of dissonance greeted Akhavan as she first began to identify as bisexual while at Smith College – which, recalling the imperative to "have a half-shaved head and a pierced septum," she experienced as "a good place to be a lesbian, a terrible place to be bisexual" (Kachka 2015).[3] Whereas anything other than straight was a "horror" on the home front, among her queer radical cohort Akhavan found herself falling short of expectations about self-presentation and resistant to claiming identity labels like *fluid* and *pansexual* and *queer*, all purportedly more progressive than the ostensibly obsolete *bisexual*. The perception of bisexuality as a hand-me-down from normative understandings of sexuality, one that simply substitutes a trichotomy (hetero/homo/bi) for the entrenched dichotomy, thereby re-inscribing dominant notions of sexuality as innate and fixed, has kept it the perennially undermined, proverbial silent letter in LGBTQ. Those identifying as bisexual typically experience the whiplash of biphobia emanating from both straight and queer constituencies, for contradictory reasons: straights are wary of bisexuality's blurring of the sexual binary, while queer discourse blames bisexuality for the binary's reinforcement.

Akhavan has openly related her own struggle with the term and its significations, admitting: "I hated coming out as bisexual. I came out as that from the get-go, but that word always felt uncomfortable. Bisexual sounds gauche and tacky … Disingenuous. Whereas there's only pride when I say lesbian, there's only coolness to say queer. Bisexual didn't feel like it represented me and I wanted to know why, when technically it very much represents who I am" (Hanna 2018). Akhavan's comments here respond not only to her own self-naming but to the word's widespread use, at the time of *Appropriate Be-*

havior's release, in press profiles and film reviews. She recalls, while travelling the world attending film festival screenings, having "heard myself described as 'the bisexual' at every other introduction" and its making "my stomach flip, in a non-fun way" (Stanford 2018). Not only would this experience provide the impetus for *The Bisexual*, it emboldened Akhavan to confront her own prejudices while striving to improve bisexuality's public image, having noted the need for more bisexual role models. "There's Tila Tequila and Anne Heche; we're not doing great," she lamented in 2015 (Akhavan and White 2015).[4] For these reasons, Akhavan has consistently if ambivalently self-identified, striving to overcome the personally and culturally imposed shame and misperception that beleaguers the bi-identified, as she suggests: "Saying you're bisexual is like saying 'I'm a huge slut.' It's so uncomfortable, and I feel very taboo calling myself bi, but it is what I am and every time I say it I'm winning a tiny victory for myself, I am going to dictate what this means, and it doesn't mean I can't make up my mind or I'm confused" (Davidson 2015). Akhavan insists here on the ongoing importance of using identity labels – against those social constructivist suspicions that they fix and universalize categories of sexual selfhood – not only for purposes of political coalition-building, but to destigmatize and redefine their meanings as always evolving, intersectional, and individualized.

It is hard to overemphasize how long-awaited and welcomed a "for us, by us" bisexual screen narrative was at the time that *Appropriate Behavior* appeared; I was both elated to discover it and regretful that it was released only just too late to have been addressed in *The B Word*. As Chloe Benson remarked in reviewing *Appropriate Behavior*, "the inimitable salience of bisexuality in Akhavan's film, its marketing, and the press that has surrounded its release" makes it a landmark – perhaps *the* landmark – work in the bisexual screen corpus (2014, 255).

Even in the brief filmography of works treating bisexuality openly and sensitively – *Sunday Bloody Sunday* (1971), *Puccini for Beginners* (2006), and *Call Me by Your Name* (2017) come most readily to mind – *Appropriate Behavior* stands out for having both its creator and protagonist explicitly voice their bisexual identity, and for its presentation of much-needed perspectives by women of colour. Whereas the overwhelming majority of bisexual characterizations onscreen have been rendered by those *not* so identifying, Akhavan's experiential understanding and firsthand view bring authenticity and insight to parsing the experiences that bisexuals share. Being on the receiving end of cultural perceptions that bisexuality is inadequately queer, Akhavan leans into this semi-exclusion from the queer club, flaunting the "B word" and resignifying it as *inappropriately* rather than inadequately queer. Having eschewed, ever since *The Slope*, the expectation that minority filmmakers create positive, palatable imagery, in *Appropriate Behavior* Akhavan continues endowing her only slightly more removed screen self with the personally and politically assailable messiness of human complexity. The resulting personification of bisexuality demonstrates both that the negative stereotyping around it is not entirely off base and yet nonetheless fails to reveal the whole story.

Switching and Straddling

As laid out in act I, Akhavan's debut success and subsequent career suggest that bisexuality's in-betweenness enables forms of code-switching and industry niche-straddling conducive to contemporary circuits of transmedia dissemination. Where there I addressed how this (self)positioning of Akhavan and *Appropriate Behavior* operated at the macro-level of film industry modes and audience targeting, here I home in on *Appropriate Behavior*'s in-betweener signalling at the micro-level of dialogue and narrative action. These text-based cues function by purposefully addressing, and accommodating, both queer and straight audiences. Much like Shirin's defining "no homo" for Maxine's (and our) benefit, as discussed in act I, this dual address informs Akhavan's choice in the meet-cute sequence to have Maxine reference the meaning of the term *gold star* (a lesbian who has never slept with a man), even as this same exchange of dialogue has Shirin sarcastically reply "Naturally" to Maxine's describing herself and her ex "going out for a couple of months, and we decided to move in together." Knowledge of the joke about lesbians bringing a U-Haul on the second date enhances one's appreciation of Shirin's sarcasm here, without confounding an unknowing viewer, as leaving "gold star" undefined would do. Similar strategies are used in crossover films like *Chasing Amy* (1997), in which the lesbian protagonist pantomimes fisting for the enlightenment of her straight pal, and *The Kids Are All Right*, when Julianne Moore's character explains lesbians' predilection for gay male porn – thus informing (even titillating) the straight audience without alienating queer viewers. Such a representational strategy is distinct from the in-the-know address aimed squarely at a queer audience, as in *Go Fish*'s butch/femme couple beginning their first date with an extended scene of nail cutting that goes wholly unexplained and presumably not understood by many straight viewers, whom this "for us, by us" film declines to acknowledge, let alone educate. Still another strategy is illustrated by *Bound* (1996), whose in-jokes are planted in plain sight – for example, Jennifer Tilly's femme Violet noting but not explaining the labrys tattoo of Gina Gershon's butch Corky by asking coyly "Are you surprised I know what it is?" – yet are couched within a film that, as its not terribly convincing butch casting indicates, hardly strives for the queer authenticity of *Go Fish*. Neither identical to nor wholly different from these cases, *Appropriate Behavior* carves out a middle road befitting its in-betweener status, engaging both queer and straight viewers, but never in a way intended to exclude either camp.

Representing bisexuality entails, then, a good deal of code-switching and shape-shifting, sometimes obligatory and at other times optional. This straddling has advantages; Shirin avails herself of femme privilege when she relies on Maxine's chivalry in buying them drugs ("You're lucky I'm so butch," says Maxine), yet it can also make for maddening instances of invisibility, as when Shirin runs into a newly coiffed Maxine and now-girlfriend Tibet at a party.

SHIRIN: Maxine and I used to be together, can you believe it?
TIBET: Nope.
SHIRIN: Why not?
TIBET: I thought you were straight.
SHIRIN: Fuck you.
MAXINE: Whoa, that was uncalled for.
SHIRIN: Your hair is uncalled for.

That Tibet's presumption provokes such anger in Shirin suggests another persistent aggravation: the assumption that femme equals straight – so pervasive, irritatingly enough, as to be voiced by an apparent lesbian so femme that she was once (as she's overly fond of mentioning) a hair model. In the "It Gets Better?" episode of *The Slope*, Akhavan had made light of this lack of visible evidence when introducing herself and Jungermann as a couple and feeling compelled to add, "Even though I don't look gay." Similarly, in their meet-cute, Shirin's immediately pegging Maxine by her soft butch swagger allows her to accurately (however inappropriately) effuse "I love dykes." Meanwhile, Shirin must not only announce herself to be bi but also profess, emboldened by drink, "I know I don't look like I'm into girls and that I was just talking about being a boner killer, but I am super sexy and super into girls."

Akhavan's fascination with rules around word usage and her fondness for irony is manifested in Shirin's semi-closeted reliance on evasive phrasing. When Shirin's father asks, "How's your love life – any boys?" Shirin responds cagily, "No boys at all." Not always so deft, Shirin later slips up in maintaining a heteronormative façade with her parents. Helping with her post-breakup move into the Brooklyn loft shared with the goth couple, Shirin's mother says optimistically, "At least you have a sexy roommate." "Felicia? I find her a bit terrifying," Shirin answers, to which her mother confusedly responds, "No, I meant the guy!"[5] Shirin similarly stumbles when her father asks why her apartment with Maxine has only one bed, offering up a conspicuously improbable excuse.

SHIRIN: It's European and thrifty. There are a lot of benefits. I have an Italian friend named Cecilia and she and her best friend shared one bed for years, and they saved so much money on rent that they were able to afford very big weddings to their boyfriends. Also, in the movie *Beaches*, these two best friends shared a bed, and it was very inexpensive.
MEHRDAD: (*in Farsi*): Italians are weird.
SHIRIN: (*in Farsi*): You're right.

With only a few lines in the film spoken in Shirin's parents' native language and translated through subtitles, this moment recalls *Annie Hall*'s meet-cute in revealing to viewers these characters' inappropriate sentiments, and uses language to hide meaning from – in this case – the uncomprehending Maxine. Also meaningful is the reference to representational effacement of lesbianism in *Beaches* (1988), whose femme-presenting leads pass (to those not wanting to view them queerly) as readily as Shirin. In another verbal sleight of hand here, the dialogue's referencing of "an Italian friend named Cecilia" name-checks Akhavan's "partner in all things except the romantic," Cecilia Frugiuele. But where dialogue and gender presentation serve to evade, the mise-en-scène reveals what goes unspoken, by borrowing *Citizen Kane*'s (1941) famous strategy of placing a bed in the shot's background to reveal the carnal nature of the relationship between the characters in the frame's foreground. The shot further communicates the effect this dissembling is having on the relationship, with a seated and foregrounded Maxine viewing Shirin's "creepy codependent relationship with her parents" at a remove from where the trio stands in the middle distance. In the exchange that follows their departure, Maxine voices her growing insistence that "You have to tell them about us," only to have Shirin dismissively apologize for her to Crystal, "Don't mind her. She's upset 'cos I'm not out to my parents," and defend herself by saying "It's a process, I'm working on it." While gazing sympathetically but not entirely forgivingly on Shirin's struggle, this scene moves the needle further towards our association of bisexuality with passing and equivocating.

"A Sexually Confused Narcissist"

Where Shirin is partially delineated according to bisexual stereotype – in being femme and not fully out – in other ways *Appropriate Behavior* diverges from stereotypical representations of bisexuality. For example, it is Maxine who cheats on Shirin, and she does so with a man. The incident, which happens in a drunken moment late into a night of Pride partying, is sexually insignificant in that it neither progresses past kissing nor undermines Maxine's lesbian identity. As she explains, with seemingly unintended perversity, "It was a man; it was like kissing a baby, just lips touching." Like Maxine's disclosing during their meet-cute of having had sex with guys, the scene counters cultural expectations – and cinema's predominant representation – that it will be the bisexual woman who proves promiscuous, unfaithful, and inevitably "led astray" by a man.

At the same time, Akhavan steers clear of a falsely egalitarian view of bisexuality as always involving attraction to men and women in equal measure. To return to Shirin's less than suave attempt to seduce gay lawyer Sasha, their outing takes a precipitous turn after Shirin announces flirtatiously, while sampling Sasha's drink, "I can tie a cherry stem in a knot with my tongue" – only to spill the entire cocktail down her front, forcing her to spend the rest of their date with wet napkins plastered to her chest and lap. "This is on me, literally and metaphorically," Shirin says, offering another mortified apology at the embarrassment she's caused by footing the bill. Sasha meets her eye to say suggestively that she "doesn't embarrass easily," to which Shirin replies, "I like that." Yet Sasha begs off shortly thereafter. Left alone to nurse her glass of "the cheapest red you've got," Shirin is asked for her assessment by a ginger-haired guy who sidles up to peruse the menu. "Alcoholic, with an oaky finish," she replies, before he introduces himself and pert girlfriend Marie, she of the latex outfit, with whom Shirin will also convincingly connect before the threesome goes south.

Figures 38–9
Background beds used to reveal carnal relations in *Citizen Kane* and *Appropriate Behavior*.

As I discuss in *The B Word*, the threesome serves so handily as scintillating shorthand for bisexuality that the two have been representationally conflated: you rarely see one without the other (2013, 37–40). This scenario, which invariably features two women and one man, offers an easy solution to the otherwise elusive problem of how to represent bisexuality. Even when an actual ménage à trois does not come about, there typically exists a love triangle both to stand in for what goes unconsummated and to establish bisexuality as a liminal, temporary phase – so often that we can refer to the "triangle film" as a distinct narrative mode. As mentioned in act I, *Appropriate Behavior* promises the (vicarious) satisfactions of triangularity with the enticing image used as its promotional one-sheet, only to throw cold water on the typical titillations of the threesome by having it go so cringingly flat. What winds up registering is not bisexuality's interchangeability with the typical clichés of promiscuity and capriciousness, but the simultaneous insider-outsider positioning I previously termed *(non)belonging*. The threesome, then, becomes here another bisexual trope that Akhavan deploys only to puncture our expectations when it forces us to confront, rather than confirm, bisexual stereotype.

Based on the track record of sexual encounters that *Appropriate Behavior* shows, Shirin seems to connect, both erotically and emotionally, more with women than men. Yet when she finally works up the nerve to come out to brother Ali near film's end, with only slight wavering does she claim herself to be bi.

> SHIRIN: My old roommate Maxine and I were in a relationship.
> ALI: Ah, so you're a lesbian.
> SHIRIN: I was pretty into all the guys I was with, so I think I'm bisexual.
> ALI: And that's a thing?
> SHIRIN: I'm afraid so. How do you think Mom and Dad are going to take it?
> ALI: You're not gonna tell them now that it's over?!

Though sibling rivalry as much as outright biphobia informs this exchange, Ali's response dismisses Shirin's bisexuality as ending along with the relationship, and so repeats monosexist presumptions (that bisexuality is really lesbianism, nonexistent, just a phase) and casts her as a "sexually confused narcissist." That we are asked, as Ali is, to take Shirin's word for it despite no legible evidence beyond fleeting lust (for BrooklynBoy82) risks raising our, like Ali's, skepticism. In so doing, Akhavan challenges viewers to accept Shirin's self-description, no matter how qualified or contingent, and without narrative substantiation of the sort we might expect. By insisting that we take Shirin at her word – and having her voice that word explicitly – *Appropriate Behavior* hardly undermines the pleasure she (as well as lesbian viewers) takes in seeming sapphically inclined. Nevertheless, the film and its protagonist proclaim themselves as bona-fide bisexual. Shirin similarly refuses erasure as bisexual by claiming that identity as both her impulse and her right, regardless of the details of her sexual history; she insists that personal and political identity are not reducible to erotic or emotional desire.

Having regularly taught *Appropriate Behavior* since its release (in courses on queer cinema, romantic comedy, and women filmmakers), I find students largely sympathetic to Shirin's reluctance to come out to her parents, reading her not (as Maxine does) as "a closet case" but to be taken at her word when she says, "I'm waiting for the right time to bring it up, out of respect for them." Perhaps partly owing to younger generations' adherence to decrees of cultural relativism and partly to the lessened political urgency around coming out nowadays, they express opposition to Maxine's insistence that Shirin do so – at least on a timetable that Maxine dictates. Less agreement greets the question of whether Shirin's being closeted fatally undermines Shirin and Maxine's viability as a couple. On that question, Maxine attempts to have, if not the final, at least a conclusive word.

"Just a Phase"

As with Akhavan's reflecting, in the quotation that begins act I, on the power inherent in words, Maxine's stinging dismissal of bisexuality as "just a phase" becomes the tipping point past which the couple cannot recover. In its first use, this phrase signifies Shirin's wishful thinking that her and Maxine's sex life will rebound, as well as (I've suggested) nodding to *Annie Hall*. Hearing it a second time in *Appropriate Behavior* sounds the relationship's death knell. To make one final comparison between these films, their respective break-up scenes provide, for me, the clearest sign of the power of Akhavan's revisionist reimagining of Allen's now-classic work.

Whereas Alvy and Annie's relationship comes to an amicable stall ("I think what we've got on our hands is a dead shark"), the post-birthday scene in which Maxine cuts up Shirin's underwear and she retaliates by breaking liquor bottles, along with the scene of their post-Pride fight in the street, are wrenching to watch. These scenes' severity distinguishes *Appropriate Behavior* from *Annie Hall* and the vast majority of romantic comedies (radical or not, queer or not, uncoupling or not). Even before Maxine hurls her vindictive final blow, these scenes stand out partly for daring to show queer women duking it out as any contentious couple might, but mostly because (whether or not you root for them), it's troubling to see onetime sweethearts descend to treating each other so viciously. Having felt stymied while a NYU film student by her own self-critical habit of asking "What would Noah [Baumbach] do?" (Ehrlich 2014), with these sequences Akhavan rivals those of spousal vitriol presented five years later in Baumbach's *Marriage Story* (2019), and vies with those in another she has named as an inspiration: Ingmar Bergman's masterwork of marital dissolution, *Scenes from a Marriage* (1974), initially the model for *Appropriate Behavior*.

In defiance of Maxine's belittling blow, "Don't bother telling your parents about us," Shirin does so, albeit inconclusively and not in time to save her relationship with Maxine. This moment does not, in other words, have the pivotal or revelatory weight it typically bears in the coming-out narrative. Shirin chooses deliberately ambiguous wording when she confesses to her mother, who is administering first aid to the burn resulting from Shirin's flubbed fire-jumping at the second Nowruz celebration, "Mom, I'm a little bit gay." Her mother responds in Farsi, "No, you're not," in another momentary shift of language for the purpose of disavowing queerness. Shirin insists, "Yes I am, and I was in love with Maxine." Her mother merely shushes her, no longer trusting language to keep the truth veiled. The scene ends there, its inconclusiveness denying the coming-out scene its accustomed finality; it suggests rather that coming out is an ongoing process – with flubs and burns along the way – that does not necessarily result in the stark alternatives of rejection or acceptance presented in more conventional narratives. What's important here is Shirin's having finally voiced her personal declaration – rather than her family's acceptance, or that of the broader community group that in so many films is conveniently on hand to provide public acknowledgment and affirmation.

Later that night, lying awake in her childhood bed, Shirin gets up and crosses the hall to her parents' room, where she stands in the doorway watching them sleep until her mother stirs and asks if she's okay. "I'm okay," Shirin answers, staying put. Unlike their forced proximity within the same frame during Shirin's previous visit to the family home, a shot-reverse set-up now positions her at a less "codependent" remove, occupying her own frame, her stance at their bedroom's threshold an apt marker of her ongoing progress. Shirin wears an oversized shirt on which is printed "A Century of Women on Top: Smith College Centennial 1875–1975"; its feminist messaging, complete with sexual innuendo, marks another defiant step away from familial and cultural silencing. This moment also highlights a pronounced and purposeful slippage between filmmaker and character, wherein knowing Akhavan's alma mater and experience there of having been judged "not gay enough" invites us to read Shirin's wearing this shirt at this moment to be her *self*-determination of queer belonging (even without a shaved head and

Figure 40
Akhavan as Shirin, forcing her family to confront her sexually liberated self.

septum piercing). Predictably, her mother's only response to Shirin's lingering is to request that she "stop breathing so loud," another deflection but one to which Shirin doesn't contribute, and one more true to life for being, like Akhavan's own family history, a work in progress. "She knows for sure what's up," Shirin subsequently reports to Crystal, vowing, "I'm going to bring it up in about a month." "I'm proud of you," Crystal replies.

Following Shirin's coming out to her mother, another telling use of nondiegetic music – the hit single "Gole Yahk" by Iranian guitar god Kourosh Yaghmaei, a political dissident whose music was banned for decades – carries us into the next and penultimate scene. Melding balladry inspired by eleventh-century Persian poetry with 1970s psychedelic rock of the secular West, the song, whose Farsi lyrics describe a love that endures through bitter winters, trails Shirin beyond her childhood home and along a city block to suggest the resilience of both her cultural-familial ties and her spirit. Having not quite succeeded, at the previous night's Nowruz, in the fire jumping ritual by which (as Shirin glibly summed up to Maxine the year before) "you're supposed to exorcise yourself of evil spirits and start the new year fresh," Shirin performs her own exorcism by tossing the strap-on into the trash – and not, this time, looking back. As authenticator of queerness for Shirin as well as the film – not unlike the nail-cutting scene in *Go Fish*, it goes unexplained but assumed that in-the-know viewers understand its significance – in finally parting with it, Shirin in no way confirms that the relationship was "just a phase," she only acknowledges its end. For Shirin and Maxine, then, the strap-on replaces the straight – or homonormative – couple's engagement diamond and wedding bands, and its abandonment constitutes a queering of the uncoupling comedy's by-now-clichéd scene of the newly (or not so newly) singleton unshackling herself from a defunct relationship. Like Shirin's coming out, it is not a final act, but it is a bold act nonetheless, and a first step into whatever the future holds.

Finale
The Bisexual and Beyond

That *Appropriate Behavior* should be so widely admired upon release but lead to a self-imposed fallow period in which, Akhavan recalls, "I was being sent scripts that were really big-budget, shittier versions of the film I had already made," had her worrying in print about the "second-film slump" known disproportionately to afflict women filmmakers. The challenge of finding exposure beyond the festival circuit brought into focus the triple threat long faced by women filmmakers: of joining the ranks of the "one and done," of having a second feature go south and ending up in "director jail," or of being confined to a genre ghetto. Vowing to wait for something worthwhile to come along, Akhavan eventually found it in adapting Emily Danforth's YA novel *The Miseducation of Cameron Post*, a project partner Cecilia Frugiuele brought her and insisted she make. The film, released in 2018 and awarded the Sundance Grand Jury Prize, is a queer coming of age story set in the 1990s, which stars Chloë Grace Moretz as a teen sent unwillingly to gay conversion therapy – a practice that unfortunately persists to this day, such that a review upon the film's release referred to it as "Mike Pence's Worst Nightmare" (Ehrlich 2018). Managing to be both politically noble (despite Akhavan's expressed aversion to virtue-signalling) and professionally savvy (for showing her range), while also conveying (and eliciting) the genuine feeling of her more autobiographically inspired work, it stands as an admirable second feature even if it failed to deliver the career boost she had sought. "Winning an award at Sundance for *The*

Miseducation of Cameron Post did nothing for my life, except it really gave me a sense of entitlement," Akhavan reflects. "I think most women don't have that innate sense of entitlement that most men are born with, especially when they work in male-dominated industries. I'm really grateful for that: My own feeling of 'I deserve the world'" (Stanford 2018).

Worthy projects were nonetheless not immediately forthcoming in the wake of *Appropriate Behavior* and, lured by television's proliferating opportunities at a time of contraction in the indie film economy, Akhavan again drew on personal experience in developing the idea for a series. Akhavan describes being motivated by her repeated, reductive labelling in the media upon *Appropriate Behavior*'s release, recalling, "I didn't mind that they were calling out my sexuality but there was something about being called a bisexual publicly – even though it's 100 per cent true! – that felt totally humiliating and in bad taste, and I wanted to understand why" (Press 2018). Developing the project at the Sundance Episodic Labs in 2014, she then pitched a series premised on the question "What if a lesbian did the worst thing in the world a lesbian could do, and became interested in men?'" to several major US studios, all of whom passed, offering excuses that "they already had a gay series, or a series starring a brown woman, or [so said Amazon] *Transparent* [2014–19]" although "nobody had a Middle Eastern show," Akhavan (2018) noted wryly. Having gotten no bites stateside, Akhavan impulsively relocated to London, where Frugiuele was living, and together they landed a production deal for a six-episode series with Channel 4, which released *The Bisexual* in the UK in the fall of 2018 and collaborated with Hulu for US distribution shortly thereafter.

In the series, Akhavan plays an American in London who, after ending a decade-long relationship with her girlfriend–business partner (played by Maxine Peake), starts dating men. The series extends the navigation of bisexuality's thorny terrain initiated in *Appropriate Behavior*, a terrain that, as Akhavan found, remains contested and provocative: "I definitely had to defend making this series because it was so taboo. It was lesbians in my life who said 'that's inherently offensive – the narrative of a woman leaving a woman and dating men is just wrong.' I want to know 'Why is it wrong?' We're not saying one is better than the other. It's just the truth of this woman's sexuality, that she's been denying and wants to explore" (Harris Green 2019). It's testament to Akhavan's artistic growth that the series strives for more inclusive representation than its title suggests. It does so by following *both* women's post-breakup reckonings with the inconvenient truths that their decade of monogamy has masked, and furthermore explores different experiences of queerness among characters whose age range spans three decades. The series gives more weight still to the complications of reconciling one's sexuality with one's familial-cultural heritage, and aspires even further in its intersectional attention to the socioeconomic and systemic barriers to (queer women of colour especially) experiencing sexuality as a choice. Lacking the space to do the series justice, I offer simply my enthusiastic recommendation and reassurance that, for those concerned Akhavan's sensibility might be growing overly serious, the ending of *The Bisexual* shows that she hasn't lost her taste for fart jokes.

Unfortunately, it appears no second season is forthcoming. While initially disappointed, I have come to think it for the best. While Akhavan reports that the experience of making the series was difficult, and its reception has in my view been inadequate to its achievement, the six episodes (as I aim to demonstrate elsewhere [2020b, 233–43; forthcoming]) constitute an enormously valuable contribution to the still lamentably small library of authentic representations of bisexuality. In the interim since, Akhavan has relocated back to Brooklyn and through the 2020–21 pandemic was working on a book of personal essays tentatively titled *Late Bloomer* (which, in its double meaning as a professional self-description, is somewhat puzzling given that she made her first feature by thirty). Another exciting and highly personal project is underway, which I'll leave to her to describe in our reprinted dialogue to follow. She has also named as her dream project "a Disney or Marvel movie," and with the glass ceiling finally broken on both it's no longer unimaginable that she might finally get her wish (Stanford 2018).[1] I for one am excited to see what the first Iranian bisexual princess or superhero can do.

As for dream projects, I would be remiss not to express that writing this book has been, for me, precisely that. As Dina Iordanova (2016) has observed, "Academic work is at its most vital when life experience informs its emphases and concerns." Having devoted so many hours, days, years to thinking and writing about the often disavowed, frequently disappointing, and invariably fleeting instances of bisexuality onscreen, I found in *Appropriate Behavior* that thrilling sensation of finally feeling represented. Judging from what I've come to know are its inconspicuous yet deeply invested ranks of fans – a description one could apply also to bisexuals – I doubt very much I'm alone in that feeling of being seen, or in my certainty that I'll be rewatching *Appropriate Behavior* for years to come. In my estimation, that certifies it as a queer film classic.

Having had three acts in which to express my admiration and fondness for *Appropriate Behavior*, I turn now to what we might call the encore, which was for me also nothing short of dream-fulfilling: a discussion with the film's creator. I can't help but think it's either divine providence, the anxiety of influence, or Akhavan's sublime wit, but her response to learning of this book was a (characteristically self-effacing) paraphrasing of *Annie Hall*'s opening monologue ("Annie and I broke up, and I still can't get my mind around that") that nonetheless managed, also characteristically, to make it her own: "I can't really wrap my brain around this … wow" (Desiree Akhavan, email to author, 21 April 2020). With appreciation for her having graciously agreed to be interviewed, what follows is a condensed and edited version of our conversation.

Encore

"A Sociopath Who Keeps a Low Overhead"

The following conversation between Desiree Akhavan (DA) and the author (MSF) took place via Zoom on 29 July 2020.

MSF: First, how are you doing? How has the whole world falling apart and film culture going totally virtual been for you?

DA: I'm trying to think of how to sum it up … This period has taught me a lot about myself – more specifically my loneliness and my goals, and how I think I made my job not just my identity, but my home. Ever since I finished making *The Bisexual*, I've been trying to figure out what I need to be happy. I think that this moment in time has given me some perspective on the things that were making me unhappy. The work can be your identity, but it can't be your everything. For the past decade I've been so busy chasing success that I never recognized it when it came to me. I think, moving forward, I'm slightly better equipped after all this time alone to recognize and appreciate good things when they're happening to me.

MSF: I'm glad to hear that. That really speaks to a lot of what I've been going through too, so it's always nice to hear that you're not alone.

DA: You feel like your work identity is everything about you?

MSF: Oh yeah, it's been my whole identity for a long time … And I love my work, as I'm sure you do too … On to *Appropriate Behavior*, your DP [director of photography] Chris Teague is a man, but there were a number of women on the crew; I'm sure a lot of queer folx as well. How do you think about questions of the male gaze, the female gaze, the queer gaze, specifically as it relates to cinematography, and to working with your crew?

DA: I was very lucky to have made that film with Chris, who really held my hand through the shoot – I was incredibly green and overwhelmed. I'd heard really good things about [him] from my friend Markus Kirschner (who ended up production designing *The Miseducation of Cameron Post*) as well as Liz Holm, who'd just done *Obvious Child* [2014] with him. Chris is incredibly talented, patient, and smart. He really got to know me and my point of view. Looking back, I can't believe how lucky I was to find a partner who was both experienced and respectful. It's especially rare to find in a cis male DP. I hit the jackpot with Chris. He was really sensitive to the fact that I was starring in the film. I've seen a lot of men overpower someone who's a beginner. They see what they perceive to be weakness and then step in to "help." Chris understood that there's more than one way to lead, and it's not always by throwing your weight around. Sometimes it's with vulnerability. He always kept me in the driver's seat and found ways to support my vision.

We watched films together while we prepped. We talked about what spoke to us in our favourite scenes. We watched *Margot at the Wedding* [2007], we watched Woody Allen. I really love the film *Fat Girl* – we watched that. I love where the camera is placed. *Margot at the Wedding* in particular has really dynamic coverage with good movement. So does *Husbands and Wives* [1992]. It was looking at where has the camera been strategic?

But then, the truth is, once you're on set, everything goes out the window. You're moving so fast; especially with a movie at that budget level, being on set is just problem-solving. It's looking around with your heads of department, and saying these are the ingredients in the fridge, what can we make for dinner? We've got those emergencies there, we've got that fire there, everything's going crazy, that cop is breathing down our neck. What can we shoot in the allotted time? How many angles can I get here before I'm kicked out at this location?

It was a real collaboration between myself, [producer] Cecilia Frugiuele, Chris Teague, and [production designer] Miren Marañón [Tejedor]. It was all of us working together to try to piecemeal something from nothing. And I don't think we went in with a particularly queer gaze, as much as it was like a cheap gaze (*laughs*). We had no time or money. And we were just trying to get by.

Actually, my editor Sara Shaw is queer and entirely shaped the final product, so there you go: queer gaze intact.

MSF: That was actually my next question: the nonlinear editing. At what point did you decide to structure the script that way? To bring up the dreaded Woody Allen question, how did *Annie Hall* emerge in your conception [of *Appropriate Behavior*] and how did it inform your writing, or your shooting and editing?

DA: Isn't it so funny how powerful a decade is? Recently, in quarantine, I have been coming face to face with a lot of films I cut my teeth on like *Jules et Jim* [1962] and *Manhattan* [1979].

MSF: Polanski maybe?

DA: I haven't rewatched *Knife in the Water* [1962] yet. I'm really scared. (*laughs*) 'Cos I loved it. That was the film [of his] that I really loved.

MSF: It's such a model for how to make a low-budget film with very few resources.

DA: Exactly. I think we have eyes now and I'm grateful. And I can't tell if it's because I'm thirty-five and not twenty-five. Or if it's because of the world we're living in right now, but I have this awareness and this self-esteem that I didn't have before, when I was like, "Well, them's the rules." Noah Baumbach was one of the voices that I felt was my voice. I'm Iranian, I'm gay, I'm not you, but you have my voice in your body. That's crazy.

MSF: What do you think it was about that voice that you heard, what was the sensibility that you were channelling?
DA: I think it's being bitter, lonely, and a bit deadpan.

MSF: In thinking about *Annie Hall* in relation to your film, I see [*Annie Hall*] staying on the surface of the comic, the light, the distanced, while *Appropriate Behavior* has the deadpan, the irony, but you're willing to dip into unabashed intimate emotional scenes. How do you determine how to balance that?
DA: It's not strategic and I'm not sure I do balance it. *Appropriate Behavior* is my attempt at light and fluffy. I wish it were lighter.

MSF: There's no such thing as too dark for me. I mean, I love *Fat Girl* as well.
DA: I'm so happy to hear that you love *Fat Girl*.

MSF: But you do still make the choice not to represent your feelings at arm's length; you do open yourself.
DA: It's not a choice, though. I wish it were a choice. But why would you give a shit about these characters, unless there was blood on the page? It's the reason I star in it too. I'm not a great actor, but I think it's exciting as a viewer to know you're watching the person at the helm of the film who conceived of the thing saying, "This is my truth (or a version of my truth). This is my body." I think it makes the stakes higher.

[Back to your original question about Woody Allen], basically the first draft of the film was written while I was still making *The Slope*. I conceived of the film thinking that it would star me and Ingrid [Jungermann]. At first I completely lifted the structure of *Scenes from a Marriage* because I knew it would be easy to produce. I wrote the film as twelve scenes examining the rise and fall of a relationship over the course of the year. I imagined I'd take out a

$10,000 loan and shoot a scene a month for a year, editing and producing it one month as a time. Then, my relationship with Ingrid started deteriorating and it became clear we wouldn't be able to work together any longer.

I shared the script with Cecilia, asking for her thoughts and advice as my friend. She read it and proposed that we make it together, with her producing. From there, we started developing the script. She started giving me assignments like, "write a scene about your family." She asked the right questions. I started writing more scenes, but I still had these scenes that I loved from the previous script, like when they meet on New Year's Eve, and when they have a fight on Maxine's birthday, when they say I love you for the first time. All those two-hander scenes were from that original script.

I still felt ill-equipped to structure a film, so I stole the structure off *Annie Hall*. I realized I was creating a love story about a couple that doesn't end up together, and that you should know from the first minute that they're not going to be together. And that's when *Annie Hall* came into play. You know from the beginning of that film, it's the first thing he says: "Annie and I broke up." And then it goes back in time. I thought, "Oh, that would be a perfect rip off. Why don't you just make that film again?" (*laughs*). Laziness and lack of experience accounts for a lot of my creative choices.

MSF: And the anxiety of influence that beleaguers us all. But in the best cases you make something even better, or at least as good as what you're borrowing from?

DA: I have never had qualms about stealing. I came of age reading *Hitchcock/Truffaut*, and feeling that to steal is a part of art. To reinterpret is the way things move on and advance. I never felt weird about it, and I still don't feel weird about it.

MSF: With the autobiographical instincts that you bring and the willingness to lean into what's uncomfortable and to really explore it, I want to ask you about bisexuality. You've been making work and putting it out there for about a decade now, so how has your thinking about bisexuality changed? How are you thinking about what you've said is your feeling that you need to say the word [bisexuality], that the word needs to be used?

DA: I think the process of making the TV show [*The Bisexual*] helped me work through some shit. A lot of life is about redefining things for yourself. You come into this world and you have all these check marks: Iranian looks like *this*, a gay person looks like *this*, a bisexual *this*. Then, slowly, you can start to redefine these things for yourself based on who you are. It's the same way I think being queer is a superpower. You get to redefine what sex is, what family is.

MSF: In terms of redefining and reassessing what you're told, there are so many gay films that are coming-out movies. How are you redefining the coming-out movie with *Appropriate Behavior*? How are you thinking about coming out as a bisexual as being a specific thing unto itself?

DA: I think it's a coming-out film, but that's not the centrepiece of the film. The thesis statement is more about love lost. It's a love story, first and foremost, and coming out is a part of it. I actually think the bisexuality element of it is not a focal point of the plot or the execution. I actually got comments from bisexuals saying why isn't it more about my sexuality? Why isn't it more heavily featured and why don't we get into that conversation? It's one of those things that we gloss over in the film. And I think that's fine. I don't think it's about bisexuality.

MSF: What about your choice in *Appropriate Behavior* to present [Akhavan's character] Shirin's attraction to women versus her attraction to men? You made choices with *Appropriate Behavior* that you were going to show Shirin's relations with women and her desire for and appeal for women to be a bit more pronounced and convincing than with the guys in the film. Is that fair?

DA: That's fair.

MSF: What was your thinking about that?

DA: It's where the story took us because Shirin is in love with a woman. So we show her in love, and then we show her fucking – and her fucking is not that great, because we were being honest about what it is like to meet dudes off Tinder. It's fun for a minute, but often it's not beyond that.

In the threesome, it's strictly a story about her being more attracted to the woman than the man, but that also is a story about ego. It's not just about sexual attraction. It's about the way that men and women behave sexually and how a male ego is really fragile and delicate, and the minute that you fuck with it the boner dies and you're kicked out of the apartment. That, to me, was more about how the vibe between the two women could be. "Let's connect. It's okay if we don't fuck, if this is awkward we can move on." We're having a connection, whereas for the man in the room, if you're not going to suck my dick then please leave.

I think you feel a real responsibility as a filmmaker to champion female love and it's something we so rarely see, it definitely was something I was more excited to shoot than straight sex or straight attraction. I have seen that millions of times before, and I wasn't as interested.

MSF: Some of what I'm picking up on in *Appropriate Behavior* also has to do with the casting choices and the chemistry that you had. Not to say that the male cast also wasn't great, but I love the female cast of *Appropriate Behavior*. I mean, every last person who had the smallest number of lines ... female and male. Let me ask you about that: the casting process and how you found all of these wonderful actors with whom you shared this great chemistry and female friendship especially, whether it's the roommate or Crystal or the threesome or the Aimee Mullins character, who is such a wonderful cameo.

DA: To me, *Appropriate Behavior* is such a rookie film, I don't watch it. It makes me cringe. Recently I gave a talk and they played a scene from the film and I was dying inside.

MSF: I think by "rookie," you mean it's a first feature. Like *The 400 Blows* [1959] is a first feature; *Stranger than Paradise* [1984] is a first feature. It has that kind of raw, even amateurish character that's charming, that's about making the most out of the little that you had to work with.

DA: *Stranger than Paradise* and *The 400 Blows* are amazing. You can't compare them to this. *Appropriate Behavior* is, like, forty per cent fart jokes.

Our casting director Allison Twardziak did a fantastic job – she brought most of that cast together. The one exception is Halley Feiffer [*who plays Crystal*], who is one of my oldest friends. We met at age fourteen and wrote our first plays at the same time, which means that she started writing plays and I copied her. She was the coolest person I'd ever met. Halley introduced me to Rebecca Henderson [*who plays Maxine*], and I asked Rebecca to do a reading of a scene from the movie at NYU, where I was a grad student at the time. We did the scene where they say I love you for the first time. Allison was at that reading, and that's how we met. She put the rest of the cast together. She was really good at thinking outside the box – John Francis [Cody DeFranco] was a barista who worked at the coffee shop outside the building we were holding auditions in.

MSF: Another way you could think about *Appropriate Behavior* is that it's a romantic comedy. It's a film about love. It's a film about uncoupling rather than couple formation, which is how we usually define romcom, and why your film, like *Annie Hall*, is a "radical romantic comedy." What's your relationship with romantic comedy and how did you think about romcom, if you did, when you were making *Appropriate Behavior*?

DA: I love romantic comedies. And I think they're all lies. And I think they're really irresponsible and if I could only watch them all day I would. That's how I feel. I feel all the feelings. I feel like I was lied to, like everything I knew about sex and love, I learned from romantic comedies. I had a really naïve idea of what romantic love was. And the first time I fell in love I got engaged really quickly because I thought "Oh, we're in love and you're a good person and

I'm a good person and we'll be good together forever." And it didn't occur to me that you could change, that relationships change, that it's really hard to change together, it's really hard to stay in love. All the things, all the nuance of loving and fucking are taken out of romantic comedies and tossed on the ground and what you're left with is a puff piece. What you're left with is propaganda that life is empty without romantic fulfillment.

All of that said, the genre is so satisfying. I love love. I fall in love really hard. Over and over again. I'm realistic about [romantic comedy's] shortcomings. It's my favourite genre and I love to fuck with it. And I think having an honest perspective in this candy-coated bullshit propaganda genre is a juxtaposition that really excites me as a creator.

MSF: In addition to all the ways I've already asked you to think about *Appropriate Behavior* — as a romcom, as a queer film, as a bisexual film …
DA: I feel like we didn't talk a lot about the queer film-ness of it.

MSF: How do you see it as a queer film and how have other people seen it that way?
DA: I don't know about other people. Like, I know that it attracts a queer audience, but I will say that for me, it was really important to have those insider nods to being in a lesbian relationship. Like *Stone Butch Blues*, Bluestockings. Honestly, I'm mad at myself for not including a scene where their periods sync up. There's so much hilarious specificity that goes on when you're in a relationship with another woman that's such good fodder for comedy. And because we've seen it so rarely on screen it's all uncharted territory.

MSF: You've said in the past that you've wrestled with which words to use, who can use those words, when is it okay, when is it not okay. With regards to "the B word," not that that's a slur, but it comes already loaded with so much meaning. What are the advantages of insisting on continuing to use it? Will it lose that fraught meaning as a result?

DA: That what's hard. I wanted to continue to use it because of that fraught meaning. I think it's really exciting to reappropriate words. But what's frustrating now is because of where the conversation about gender is going – which is so great – the B word is starting to seem exclusionary of gender nonconforming folks.

MSF: That's always been a critique of that term "bisexual," rightly or wrongly, that it is gender-fetishizing in the same way that being straight or being gay is alleged to be. Not to put words in your mouth, but it sounds like what you're saying is that you're not questioning whether [the word "bisexuality"] is legit for you because it feels right to you.
DA: Well, it's not that it feels right. It's that it does have that baggage. I particularly like saying "fuck you" to the baggage.

MSF: To make sure I'm understanding, you feel like the word bisexual might have lost its legitimacy or its usefulness as a result of its being perceived as being trans-exclusionary?
DA: Potentially.

MSF: It's a tough term to wrap your head around and it's also a tough thing to represent; I'm sure I don't have to tell you that. But could you talk a bit about the challenges to representing a bisexual character or just bisexuality?
DA: I don't really know how to answer that. I will say there's the toughness of living it. I guess, I feel like I said it in [*The Bisexual*]. It does feel tacky. "It feels gauche, it feels like your genitals have no alliance, just an open door policy." I make a big speech about it in episode 3 (*laughs*). It's my own self-perpetuating insecurity and I don't want to live like that. Those aren't insecurities I carry with me at thirty-five but they were insecurities I had at thirty when I was writing *The Bisexual*.

MSF: Are there ways that representing bisexuality would be harder than representing lesbian, gay, queer with regard to things like the coming-out narrative?

DA: It would depend on your circumstances. That's why it's so hard to talk about all this. It depends on where you come from. It depends on what's around you, it depends on, like, if you're surrounded by TERF lesbians. It really is context.

MSF: Speaking of contexts and the datedness of certain words and maybe the inappropriateness of certain jokes, when you think back to *The Slope*, how do you view it now?

DA: I watched a few episodes yesterday because I'm writing a chapter in my book that covers that time period. I just kept thinking, "Wow, it's rough!" I was very green, but there were some jokes and some moments that I thought, "That's me. I would still do that." I don't remember all of it, so I don't know if there's anything offensive in there, but I think I'm cool with the politics of it. I think we say some wild things that, in the context of that show, work. I don't know. Did you catch something bad?

MSF: We met briefly [at the University of Pennsylvania] when you did a talk there, and in the introduction, they showed a clip from *The Slope*. It was a scene where you and Ingrid are talking and she says something like, "You know, lesbians don't get AIDS," badmouthing gay men ... I was just thinking in preparing for this whether that would still fly. Would you still make that choice to have that particular dialogue?

DA: Yes, because Ingrid also says "Why do butch lesbians transition? That's fucked up." And my character's like "You're jealous." And she is jealous. I actually think that is a less problematic joke than the "I'm thinking of transitioning into a woman" joke [from *Appropriate Behavior*]. I think that it's about context and Ingrid's character. Markus's character – Markus [Kirschner], who plays the gay man, who was the production designer on *Cameron Post* – is saying horrible things about lesbians. I mean, it's not as rough as AIDS, he doesn't have that ammo that she does to say something quite so offensive. It's satire and you're not supposed to be on her side.

MSF: So it's about her being the one who is in this case punching down and we recognize that. She's the ultimate butt of the joke.
DA: You know, that was one of the episodes I watched yesterday and I did one of these [*pulls shocked face*]. I was literally like "Would that be okay?" I actually think it might not be a joke I'd make today, but I do think it's okay.

MSF: Do you still consider yourself politically incorrect?
DA: (*long pause*) No.

MSF: Do you feel that this approach, the approach that you take in *The Slope* and that you do, to some degree, also in *Appropriate Behavior* and in *The Bisexual* where you use satire, irony, deadpan comedy, politically incorrect jokes even – is that an approach that you feel you can really stand up for, that you feel has a purpose, has a place, does something that other approaches to dealing with queer politics and queer issues couldn't?
DA: It's my voice, and I'm still honing it. I think over the years I've gotten a better awareness of how to use it strategically. It's not a tactic for me.

MSF: I want to ask about the Iranian American aspect of not only your identity but of *Appropriate Behavior*. Alongside all those other ways of thinking about it – queer film, romcom, uncoupling drama even – it's an Iranian American film. It's going to get categorized that way, it's going to get maybe even pigeonholed that way, whether you mean it to or not. Can you talk about that a bit and how you see yourself and the film existing in this Iranian American space, as diaspora cinema?
DA: It's interesting because I feel about the Iranian-ness the same way I do about the bisexuality. I made this young and it is about the things that I am.

If I could go back now, I think that there was a missed opportunity. There's so much more interesting stuff about being a child of immigrants that I hadn't quite processed yet and that isn't in the movie. I'm glad we go to Nowruz. I'm glad that we have certain relics of that moment, but it doesn't investigate and it doesn't look at what it is to be Iranian. It's like a character tic. She's culturally different, but it's beside the point. Same with her bisexuality, it's beside the point. These are details; first and foremost this is a love story. And I think at that age, first and foremost, I wanted to be the white girl lead. And I just happened to be gay. And I just happened to be Iranian. I put it in the film, but I didn't let it shine. And now, years later, I definitely feel like it was a missed opportunity and that I was suffocating the things that made me "different" from your classic romcom lead.

MSF: Why don't you think it shines? Why do you think it's beside the point? Because it seems to be a substantial part of the film, and your family and your relation to them. It's almost as if you're leaving one relationship to enter into another one, but you don't make that segue quite in time, so you sort of miss the train, so to speak.

DA: I don't have any regrets. I think those things are just not what the film's about, it's just not about being Iranian and that's okay. I wanted for someone who looked like me and was like me to have a love story, so it's there and the family is there. It's just the headlines. She's the child of immigrants. She has a brother who's a doctor. These things are the pressure factors. They add stakes to what's going on. It was all the romantic comedy elements: now we meet her family and her family happens to be Iranian. It's the same tropes.

MSF: I won't interpret the film for you. I'll save that for the book, but I will tell you …
DA: You can interpret the film for me. I'm enjoying this!

MSF: Well, I want to tell you what my students say about this particular issue because I've taught this film in my classes and students uniformly love it. We always have a really rich conversation around this question of whether Maxine is right to insist on Shirin coming out and on her terms. Is it necessary that she come out to her family? Is Shirin a sympathetic character; are we willing to understand that it's legitimately hard for her, or is she just avoiding doing what's hard and mature? And students really do take Shirin's side. To some degree that's a deck you've stacked because you're telling a story through her eyes. And it's not like they aren't giving Maxine any legitimacy, they understand why coming out is important. And why being truthful about something important in your life is going to be of benefit to the relationship. But they also feel like it's up to [Shirin] to do it in her own time.

DA: Yeah, I think ten years ago, everybody would've been like "She should come out," and I think there's a lot of sensitivity now to what it is to grow up in a different culture.

MSF: I liked what you did in *The Bisexual* about that in looking at how when the characters were born influences their thinking about being queer and about coming out, but also with the Deniz character [played by Saskia Chana], who I loved ...

DA: She's my favourite character in the show.

MSF: She's so great. I think that's really, as I said in my [*Journal of Bisexuality*] review, the love story at the centre that's, you know, not officially in the centre.

DA: I do too. I think she's the most important character in that show and that the fight that they have at the end of episode four is the most important scene in the show.

MSF: Can you talk a bit about that, about how you see that issue of coming out and of queerness still being so important to represent, but in a different way than it would have been ten years ago? Why it's still important to tell these stories? We're supposedly in this post-queer world, some say.

DA: White people say that. Queer middle-class white people say that. It's post-queer for them and they have these blinders where they think that their experience of the world is like everybody's experience of the world, but it's not.

MSF: In changing your thinking about your Iranian identity and how important it is to you and/or to your work, how does that factor? How did you go into *The Bisexual* or into this book you're writing now wanting to make that point of how queerness is different for people without white privilege or people who aren't living in a, you know, so-called democracy?

DA: Well, Deniz is a really specific example. And I don't think it was that much about Iranian-ness as much as it was about class. It felt like a perfect way to ask who can't come out and where is the conversation trickier? Deniz is responsible for her family. When they go to the hospital, she's the one translating. She's supporting them, working with them at their off-licence, her life is completely embedded in their lives. That is a different approach to family than a Western one. It felt important to have that conversation about why she felt she couldn't come out and why it's not a judgment call that anyone else can make for her. Of course you want people to live authentically, but what she says is, I have a choice of prioritizing my family over myself and that's a particularly Middle Eastern point of view.

That was the way my parents lived and I had a really hard time understanding. I had a lot of judgment for the choices they made, but I wasn't raised in Iran and they were. The show talks a lot about class and age and what the queer experience looks like for us within those different brackets.

MSF: Are you working on something, apart from the book, that has to do with the Iranian American or the Iranian experience?

DA: I'm currently co-writing a movie right now with Cecilia about a young woman's life during the Islamic Revolution.

MSF: Are there any films or artworks that you have come across that do feel like they've told that story authentically or that you do feel like kind of resembled your experience or that of your family members?
DA: I have not seen a film about the Islamic Revolution, other than *Argo* [2012]. *Under the Shadow* [2016] is a fantastic horror film that takes place during the Iran-Iraq War.

MSF: How do you feel about how everything is streaming and not theatrically exhibited, how has that affected your career? How has it affected how you think people are experiencing your work?
DA: It's probably helped my career, a lot. I don't think that my work with the lack of movie stars in it would attract big numbers. And I also think the nature of being gay, a lot of people are closeted and find things through backwards channels. I think it's been great for me and also I don't want to hold on to the past. The world is changing, content is changing, the way we make content is changing, the way we digest content is changing, the internet is changing. I think it's my job to shift and pivot and go with it.

MSF: So you're writing a book!
DA: I'm writing a book!

MSF: Will you tell me a little about it?
DA: When I started writing I thought that it would be like, you know, Tina Fey's book – essays that were short, funny anecdotal stories about my life. And in the process of making it I've uncovered that the funniest stories in my life are actually incredibly dark. But as you said in the beginning, I do play with dark subject matter and that's sort of on-brand for me so I don't know why I'm surprised. The last month I've been writing about bulimia and it's hard to write about bulimia. It's hard to think [of] jokes. It's hard to make it a cute Tina Fey–style essay when it's something so ugly. I've been trying to find a way to make cute Tina Fey–style essays about, you know, losing my virginity to a cokehead I met in a support group for cutters. (*laughs*)

MSF: I can't wait to read it, I really can't. (*laughing*) But that's the thing about writing a memoir, you know, things keep happening to you and you keep uncovering the old stuff that you didn't want to uncover and so it's going to get longer and it's going to be later and at some point, you just have to stop writing, I guess.

DA: Exactly. And it's also like what's your perspective on the past? And every year it keeps shifting and what's the most interesting angle to take? I think that's what's hard. Even trying to write about *Appropriate Behavior*; I want to write about the making of that film, and I don't know the right way to do it. When we were editing it felt like we had nothing, and Sara [Shaw], my editor, was just convinced no one would ever watch it. And so was I. And after I watched the first cut, I wrote Cecilia this really long email that said "I'll never regret trying. But I think we need to find another line of work. And also, I'm sorry. You took such a huge risk on me and I failed you. This is legitimate bad. Please forgive me." (*laughs*) It was a really dramatic message. She responded, "One day we will frame this email."

MSF: That's a great answer. And then Sundance called.

DA: It was shocking. Nothing could have been more shocking to me than that call. I think it needed someone to champion it; someone legit to say this is a voice. If I didn't have that that seal of approval, I think that the film might have disappeared or have been viewed through a different lens.

MSF: Yeah, you needed an audience and the kind of festival sensibility that appreciated it.

DA: Who saw the potential – who said, this is cheap. This is weird. But also, it's trying something interesting.

MSF: You said before that you cringe thinking about it or watching it. But do you think that you were accurately assessing it when you say now that it was legit bad or do you think that you had been kind of internalizing that thought

because it hadn't immediately taken off or gotten into every festival or gotten a lot of financing or whatever kind of markers of its not being a success?
DA: I think it did really well for what it is; I think I was very lucky for what it is. I think that there are messy elements in it and I don't think I'm the best actress, but it has heart and when it's funny, it's funny and when it's bad, it's bad. And the threesome sequence remains my favourite thing I've ever filmed.

MSF: On that note, I'm really happy that you reminded me of the image that very obviously should adorn the cover of this book, which is the one used for the publicity – did you choose it?
DA: I did choose it. It was that or this giant 60-foot version of me photoshopped sitting on the top of the Brooklyn Bridge. (*poses with head in hands*)

MSF: Thinker pose?
DA: 100 per cent. I really struggle with key art and it's something that I've not gotten right in any of my work. I think the *Cameron Post* poster sells a different film than what we made and I feel the same way about *The Bisexual*.

MSF: For *Cameron Post*, you're talking about the one with the three kids in the back of the pickup or the tight image on Chloë [Grace Moretz]'s face?
DA: Neither of those I think captures the energy of that movie. And then I love the broken-up font on *The Bisexual*, but I don't think I got the image right.

MSF: I love the image of the three kids in the back of the pickup; I don't know if it's intentional or one of those unconscious influences, but it serves as a nice bridge from the end of *But I'm a Cheerleader*, which your film obviously has some interesting parallels or mirror image relationship with. Both sets of characters ride off into the sunset, in the back of a pickup, leaving their gay conversion camp. They get to have their big romcom moment but with no crowd applauding them.

DA: I forgot that. That's so wild. I purposely avoided watching that film again. I saw it when I was twenty and then I didn't want it in my head when we were making the film.

MSF: Do you think going forward, you would like to work again in adapting other source material, making it your own, bringing light to something that not everyone knows about as a way to celebrate what you love?
DA: For sure.

MSF: You spoke about the so-called "second-film slump" – women directors, even if their first project, as yours was, is celebrated and even profitable, still finding it hard to get a second project off the ground. Now that you're at this mid-career point, even if you're still youthful, it's been ten years and you've entered into this new phase of your career. How is it different now, if at all?
DA: I've been doing this longer, I know more than I used to. I believe in the inevitability of my success, even if I'm not 100 per cent sure what the path is.

In terms of why the second-film slump happens, it's so many reasons, but also it's privilege. I had the privilege to sleep on Cecilia's couch and write *Cameron Post* on spec. We didn't get paid to write it, and we flew ourselves out to LA to pitch it. I lived on very little for very long. Not many people can get by making so little. This work isn't stable or consistently lucrative. It's a glorified hobby for rich people and sociopaths (I'm a sociopath who keeps a low overhead).

MSF: It is unclear what indie film's going to become not only because of the changes in the industry but the world as well. What is independent cinema going to be? We don't have to answer that question today.
DA: Nobody knows how to monetize indie movies. There's just no guarantee for what works and what doesn't work and how to go about financing things. The rules are always changing. And there's a lot of fear in the room right now. I think you can work easily if you're willing to compromise on every element

Figures 41–2
Riding off into uncertain sunsets: the final shots of *But I'm a Cheerleader* and *The Miseducation of Cameron Post*.

of it and just be a director for hire. But it's hard if you have a strong point of view. You pay to play. Most directors I know dance back and forth between paid work TV directing and that kind of stuff and making the personal work that that they want to.

MSF: But you opted for another path where you're really doubling down on the stuff that you want to make, knowing that you might not be as prolific?
DA: I directed three episodes of TV last year. [Akhavan also directed two episodes of the first season of the HBO Max series *Hacks* in 2021.] And that's how I've been supporting myself lately. It was pretty miserable. I would like to be more prolific. I'm still figuring it all out.

Oh Shadow

Juan Boscán Almogávar (c. 1490–1542)

Like one receiving pleasure from a dream,
his pleasure thus proceeding from delusion,
so does imagination with illusions
conceive in vain its happiness in me.
No other good's inscribed on my sad heart,
except what in my thoughts I might procure;
of all the good I ever have endured,
what lives is only the imagined part.
My heart is frightened to proceed ahead,
seeing that its pain in ambush lies;
and so after a moment it turns back
to contemplate those glories that have fled.
Oh, shadow of relief, that fickle flies,
to make what's best in me be what I lack!

Translation © 1995 Alix Ingber

Notes

Act One

1. For more on LGBTQ+ festivals, see Richards (2017). For a discussion of digital distribution of sapphic-themed films circa 2014, see Beirne (2014, 129–38).
2. Akhavan's parents and older brother immigrated from Iran to the US shortly before Akhavan was born in 1984 in New York City. Akhavan uses "Persian" and "Iranian" interchangeably in referring to her family's pre–Islamic Republic national heritage and diasporic identity.
3. *High Art* and *Appropriate Behavior* owe much of their look to their directors of photography; Akhavan's collaborator was Chris Teague, known for lensing Gillian Robespierre's films.
4. It seems possible that *Appropriate Behavior*'s Maxine was named in part as an homage to Guinevere Turner's character (who goes by Max) in *Go Fish*, but is likely also an allusion to the affectionate name that Alvy and pal Rob (Tony Roberts) call one another in *Annie Hall*. It may also be that Shirin is in reference to renowned Iranian-born visual artist Shirin Neshat.
5. *Obergefell v. Hodges* is the landmark 2015 ruling by the US Supreme Court that the constitutional right to marry is guaranteed to same-sex couples.

6 That I have needed to insert "bisexual" into Halberstam's sentence is indicative of the effacement that bisexuality endures even within queer discourse, about which more to come in act III.
7 Act III revisits Akhavan's thesis film *Nose Job* and its real-life inspiration; Akhavan spoke openly about her stint in rehab while doing press for *The Miseducation of Cameron Post*, having found the experience informative for her thinking about that story's setting within the world of gay conversion therapy.

Act Two

1 *Annie Hall* is also arguably one of the least "his" among Allen's fifty-plus films to date, having shared screenplay credit with Marshall Brickman on this and three other occasions: *Sleeper* (1973), *Manhattan* (1979), and *Manhattan Murder Mystery* (1993).
2 In addition to *Annie Hall*, notable "uncoupling comedies" of the era include *Girlfriends* (1978), *Private Benjamin* (1980), *Rich and Famous* (1981), *Shampoo* (1975), and *An Unmarried Woman* (1978).
3 In romcom parlance, the *meet-cute* refers to the narrative trope whereby the romantic partners' first encounter conveys their compatibility and foreshadows their ultimate union, all while establishing the obstacles to coupledom that will require a feature-length narrative's worth of blocking forces and verbal sparring to overcome.
4 So Mayer surmises that BrooklynBoy82 fails to get it up on account of having over-imbibed; while the sequence leaves their encounter open to interpretation on this count, I appreciate Mayer's recognizing how all three penises with which Shirin comes into contact – those of BrooklynBoy82, the threesome's Ted, and the guy she's avoiding at the New Year's party where she meets Maxine – potentially support her self-allegation as a "boner killer" (Mayer 2017).

5 In pointing to such instances of what she calls *Appropriate Behavior*'s "citational excess," Clara Bradbury-Rance (2022) perceives the playful practice of referencing figures, movements, and texts from the past as a pronounced means by which contemporary queer feminist culture articulates and politicizes itself.
6 That Feiffer's most prominent film roles before this were as the babysitter in *You Can Count on Me* (2000) and Jesse Eisenberg's high school girlfriend in *The Squid and the Whale* (2005) contribute to this image of her as girl next door.
7 Akhavan credits editor Sara Shaw for the inspiration to use Electrelane; initially serving as temporary tracks, the songs were acquired only after the band prevailed upon their labels to make the musical rights affordable. Another featured track is by former Le Tigre member JD Samson (from her EP *MEN*), and lesbian-identified Josephine Wiggs (formerly bassist in the Breeders) composed and performed the original score.
8 Akhavan started college with the intention of studying playwriting, ending up in a cinema course having accompanied a friend who enticed her with the promise of free weed en route.

Act Three

1 *The Miseducation of Cameron Post*'s supporting characters Adam (Forrest Goodluck) and Jane (Sasha Lane), as queer people of colour, also engage these themes of entangled identity, though as Indigenous and Black/Indigenous characters/performers respectively, from perspectives more distanced from Akhavan's own.
2 Aimee Mullins is a bilateral amputee who competed in National Collegiate Athletic Association (NCAA) Division I athletics as a Georgetown University undergraduate and later in the 1996 Paralympics, both in track and field. Since retiring from competitive athletics she has served

as president of the Women's Sports Foundation, worked as a model and actor, and is a TED "All-Star" among many other accomplishments and philanthropic activities.
3 Smith College is the most politically radical of the women's college alliance known as the Seven Sisters.
4 While Tila Tequila and Anne Heche remain the most infamous bisexual celebrities, fortunately a few more aspirational figures (including Alan Cumming, Abbi Jacobson, Janelle Monáe, and Evan Rachel Wood) have emerged in the last few years.
5 Annalisa Graziano as Shirin's roommate Felicia is another standout actor who puts the perfect deadpan on her lamentably few lines ("Oh, you're on OKCupid. My taxidermist met her husband on that site").

Finale

1 While a small handful of women directors have been trusted to solo helm theatrically released Disney films – Nancy Meyers's *The Parent Trap* (1998), Angela Robinson's *Herbie Fully Loaded* (2005), and Mira Nair's *Queen of Katwe* (2016) being the most prominent to date – the higher-profile and merchandising-forward animated franchises did not gain a woman among their ranks until 2020's *Mulan*, a live-action adaptation directed by Niki Caro. Patty Jenkins's helming of DC Comics' Wonder Woman franchise (2017–) and the forthcoming *Star Wars: Rogue Squadron* (2023) has paved the way for women of colour Cathy Yan's *Birds of Prey* (2020), Gina Prince-Bythewood's *The Old Guard* (2020), and Chloé Zhao's *Eternals* (2021). While the early 2020s global pandemic and accelerating streaming wars have cast considerable uncertainty over the industry's future, the relatively robust performance of Cate Shortland's *Black Widow* upon its hybrid release in 2021 was a positive sign for Hollywood and for the future of women helming franchise action films.

References

Akhavan, Desiree. 2013. "Who Wrote It Better? Filmmaker Desiree Akhavan on the Lena Dunham Phenomenon." IFP, 21 March. https://thegotham.org/resources/who-wrote-it-better-filmmaker-desiree-akhavan-on-the-lena-dunham-phenomenon.
— 2015a. "Desiree Akhavan (Appropriate Behaviour) on High Art." BFI Flare: London LGBTQ Film Festival, 12 March. https://www.youtube.com/watch?v=fDacKuo1pgU.
— 2015b. "Desiree Akhavan's Breakthrough Breakup." *Death, Sex & Money*, WNYC, 14 January. https://www.wnycstudios.org/podcasts/deathsexmoney/episodes/desiree-akhavans-breakthrough-breakup.
— 2015c. "Desiree Akhavan on *Appropriate Behavior*." BFI National Archive, 26 March 2015. https://www.youtube.com/watch?v=3dZXEM7iq-w.
— (@akhavandesiree). 2017. (1/2) "Dear @IndieWire I love you, but saying the sex in BLUE IS THE WARMEST COLOR 'respected the essence of lesbian sex – raw, inventive, and unmatched in its intimacy' is bullshit. The sex in that film is bullshit." (2/2) "The only worse thing than the sex in that film was the abuse that director made his actors suffer in order to get such a bullshit piece of wank bank fodder. Let's stop celebrating bullshit." Twitter, 9 December, 5:07 PM. https://twitter.com/akhavandesiree/status/939617605425467397.

– 2018. "*The Bisexual.*" Talkback, NewFest, SVA Theatre, New York, NY, 29 October.

Akhavan, Desiree, and Emily Danforth. 2018. "*Miseducation of Cameron Post* Creators Take Aim at Gay Conversion Therapy." *Fresh Air*, WHYY/NPR, 25 July 2018. https://www.npr.org/2018/07/25/632242898/miseducation-of-cameron-post-creators-take-aim-at-gay-conversion-therapy.

Akhavan, Desiree, and Patricia White. 2015. "What Is Appropriate Behavior?" Dr S.T. Lee Distinguished Lecture in the Humanities, Penn Humanities Forum, University of Pennsylvania, Philadelphia, 16 September. https://vimeo.com/140859821.

Alcamo, Jess. 2014. "Appropriate Behavior – An Interview with Writer/Director Desiree Akhavan." *4:3*, 15 June. https://fourthreefilm.com/2014/06/appropriate-behavior-an-interview-with-writerdirector-desiree-akhavan/.

Bakare, Lanre. 2015. "Mark Duplass: 'There's No Excuse Not to Make Films on Weekends with Friends.'" *Guardian*, 15 March. https://www.theguardian.com/film/2015/mar/15/mark-duplass-south-by-southwest-sxsw.

Barnes, Beanie. 2014. "America's Next Wal-Mart: The Indie Film Industry." *Salon*, 21 February. www.salon.com/2014/02/22/americas_next_wal_mart_the_indie_film_industry/.

Beirne, Rebecca. 2014. "New Queer Cinema 2.0? Lesbian-Focused Films and the Internet." *Screen* 55, no. 1 (Spring): 129–38.

Bendix, Trish. 2012. "Ingrid Jungermann and Desiree Akhavan on *The Slope* and Writing Funny Lesbian Jokes." AfterEllen, 30 March. https://www.afterellen.com/people/99781-ingrid-jungermann-and-desiree-akhavan-on-the-slope-and-writing-funny-lesbian-jokes/3 - DOKXGGtj5OK2z3EU.99.

Benson, Chloe. 2017. "*Appropriate Behavior* (2014)." *Journal of Bisexuality* 17, no. 2: 251–6.

Bloom, Harold. 1997 [1973]. *The Anxiety of Influence: A Theory of Poetry*, 2nd edition. Oxford: Oxford University Press.

Bourdieu, Pierre. 1986 [1979]. *Distinction: A Social Critique of the Judgment of Taste*. London: Routledge.

Bradbury-Rance, Clara. 2022 (accepted/in press). "Appropriate Feminisms: Ambivalence and Citational Practice in *Appropriate Behavior*." *Camera Obscura* 37, no. 3: forthcoming.

Butler, Judith. 1999 [1990]. *Gender Trouble: Feminism and the Subversion of Identity*. New York: Routledge.

Christian, Aymar Jean. 2014. "Indie TV: Innovation in Series Development." In *Media Independence: Working with Freedom or Working for Free?*, edited by James Bennett and Niki Strange, 159–81. New York: Routledge.

Christian, Aymar Jean. 2018. *Open TV: Innovation Beyond Hollywood and the Rise of Web Television*. New York: NYU Press.

Danuta Walters, Suzanna. 2012. "The Kids Are All Right but the Lesbians Aren't: Queer Kinship in US Culture." *Sexualities* 15, no. 8: 917–33.

Davidson, Alex. 2015. "Bisexual Healing: Desiree Akhavan on *Appropriate Behavior*." British Film Institute, 24 June. https://www2.bfi.org.uk/news-opinion/news-bfi/interviews/bisexual-healing-desiree-akhavan-appropriate-behaviour.

Dawson, Nick. 2012. "Desiree Akhavan and Ingrid Jungermann." *Filmmaker*. https://filmmakermagazine.com/people/desiree-akhavan-and-ingrid-jungermann/#.Xvo_E_J7m8o.

Dry, Jude. 2016. "Tribeca: 'Women Who Kill' Director Ingrid Jungermann Has Some Ideas for New Queer Cinema." *IndieWire*, 15 April 2016. https://www.indiewire.com/2016/04/tribeca-women-who-kill-director-ingrid-jungermann-has-some-ideas-for-new-queer-cinema-289944/.

Duggan, Lisa. 2002. "The New Homonormativity: The Sexual Politics of Neoliberalism." In *Materializing Democracy: Toward a Revitalized Cultural Politics*, edited by Ross Castronovo and Dana D. Nelson, 175–94. Durham: Duke University Press.

Duplass, Mark. 2014. *HuffPostLive@SxSW*. 8 March. Last accessed 12 December. on.aol.com/video/mark-duplass-talks-the-reaganomics-of-the-film-industry-518150437.

Edelman, Lee. 2004. *No Future: Queer Theory and the Death Drive*. Durham: Duke University Press.

Ehrlich, David. 2014. "Sundance Director's Cut: Desiree Akhavan (*Appropriate Behavior*)." Film.com, 20 January. http://www.mtv.com/news/2772677/sundance-interview-desiree-akhavan-appropriate-behavior/.

Ehrlich, David. 2018. "'The Miseducation of Cameron Post' Review: This Beautiful Coming-of-Age Story Is Mike Pence's Worst Nightmare – Sundance 2018." *IndieWire*, 22 January. https://www.indiewire.com/2018/01/the-miseducation-of-cameron-post-review-desiree-akhavan-chloe-grace-moretz-sundance-2018-1201920629/.

Freeman, Elizabeth. 2010. *Time Binds: Queer Temporalities, Queer Histories*. Durham: Duke University Press.

Freeman, Hadley. 2015. "Desiree Akhavan on *Appropriate Behavior* and Not Being the 'Iranian Bisexual Lena Dunham." *Guardian*, 6 March. https://www.theguardian.com/film/2015/mar/05/desiree-akhavan-appropriate-behaviour-not-being-iranian-bisexual-lena-dunham.

Halberstam, Jack. 2010. "The Kids Aren't Alright!" *Bully Bloggers*, 15 July. https://bullybloggers.wordpress.com/2010/07/15/the-kids-arent-alright/

– 2011. *The Queer Art of Failure*. Durham: Duke University Press.

Halperin, David M. 1997. *Saint Foucault: Towards a Gay Hagiography*. Oxford: Oxford University Press.

Hanna, Aoife. 2018. "Who Is Desiree Akhavan? *The Bisexual* Actress May Well Look Familiar." *Bustle*, 10 October. https://www.bustle.com/p/who-is-desiree-akhavan-the-bisexual-actress-may-well-look-familiar-12208464.

Hans, Simran. 2018. "Do You Love Me Now?" *Little White Lies* no. 76 (Aug/Sep/Oct): 12–17.

Harris Green, Hannah. 2019. "Desiree Akhavan on Why TV Always Gets Bisexuality Wrong." *Studio 360*, 14 February. https://www.pri.org/stories/2019-02-14/desiree-akhavan-why-tv-always-gets-bisexuality-wrong.

Harrison, Rebecca. 2018. "Fuck the Canon (Or, How Do You Solve a Problem Like Von Trier?): Teaching, Screening and Writing about Cinema in the Age of #MeToo." *MAI: Feminism & Visual Culture*, 9 November 2018. https://maifeminism.com/fuck-the-canon-or-how-do-you-solve-a-problem-like-von-trier-teaching-screening-and-writing-about-cinema-in-the-age-of-metoo/.

Henderson, Brian. 1978. "Romantic Comedy Today: Semi-Tough or Impossible?" *Film Quarterly* 31, no. 4 (Summer): 11–23.

Himberg, Julia. 2014. "Multicasting: Lesbian Programming and the Changing Landscape of Cable TV." *Television and New Media* 15, no. 4: 289–304.

Hoberman, J. 2018. "Lucrecia Martel: A Director Who Confounds and Thrills." *New York Times*, 13 April. https://www.nytimes.com/2018/04/13/movies/lucrecia-martel-zama-argentina.html.

Hollywood Reporter Staff. 2014. "Off the Cuff: Desiree Akhavan." *A Cast*, 25 July. https://play.acast.com/s/thrpodcasts/off-the-cuff-desiree-akhavan.

Hutcheon, Linda. 1995. *Irony's Edge: The Theory and Politics of Irony*. London: Routledge.

Iordanova, Dina. "Choosing the Transnational." *Frames Cinema Journal* 9. https://framescinemajournal.com/article/choosing-the-transnational/.

Jeffers McDonald, Tamar. 2007. *Romantic Comedy: Boy Meets Girl Meets Genre*. London: Wallflower.

Kachka, Boris. 2015. "Desiree Akhavan Wants to Move Beyond the 'Bisexual Persian Lena Dunham' Tag." *Vulture*, 11 January 2015. https://www.vulture.com/2015/01/desiree-akhavan-girls-appropriate-behavior.html.

Kang, Inkoo. 2015. "*Appropriate Behavior* Review: Desiree Akhavan's Hilarious Comedy Heralds an Essential New Voice." *Wrap*, 14 January. https://www.thewrap.com/appropriate-behavior-review-desiree-akhavan-scott-adsit-girls/.

Kermode, Jennie. 2015. "Sex, Lies and Cinema: Desiree Akhavan on *Appropriate Behavior*." *Eye for Film*, 24 June 2015. https://www.eyeforfilm.co.uk/feature/2015-06-24-interview-with-desiree-akhavan-about-appropriate-behaviour-feature-story-by-jennie-kermode.

King, Geoff. 2014. *Indie 2.0: Change and Continuity in Contemporary American Indie Film*. New York: Columbia University Press.

Krutnik, Frank. 1998. "Love Lies: Romantic Fabrication in Contemporary Romantic Comedy." In *Terms of Endearment: Hollywood Romantic Comedy of the 1980s and 1990s*, edited by Peter William Evans and Celestino Deleyto, 15–36. Edinburgh: Edinburgh University Press.

Lauria, Peter. 2013. "The Box Office Gross of Every Woody Allen Movie Adjusted for Inflation." *BuzzFeed*, 2 August 2013. https://www.buzzfeed news.com/article/peterlauria/the-box-office-gross-of-every-woody-allen-movie-adjusted-for.

Levine, Nick. 2015. "Desiree Akhavan Q&A on *Appropriate Behavior*, Sex Scenes and Changing How Marginalised Communities Are Depicted in Film." *NME*, 5 March 2015. https://www.nme.com/blogs/nme-blogs/desiree-akhavan-qa-on-appropriate-behaviour-sex-scenes-and-changing-how-marginalised-communities-are-17916.

Liebenson, Donald. 2017. "The *Annie Hall* That Might Have Been: Inside Woody Allen's *Anhedonia*." *Vanity Fair*, 20 April 2017. https://www.vanity fair.com/hollywood/2017/04/annie-hall40th-anniversary-woody-allen-carol-kane-marshall-brickman.

Love, Heather K. 2015. *Feeling Backward: Loss and the Politics of Queer History*. Cambridge: Harvard University Press.

Mayer, So. 2015. *Political Animals: The New Feminist Cinema*. London: I.B. Tauris.

— 2017. "In Praise of Soft Cock." *cléo: a journal of film and feminism* 5, no. 1. cleojournal.com/2017/04/20/praise-soft-cock/.

McDermott, Catherine. 2018. "Contemporary Femininities after Postfeminism: Genre, Affect, Aesthetics." Doctoral thesis, PhD, Manchester Metropolitan University.

Merry, Stephanie. 2015. "*Appropriate Behavior* Movie Review: Desiree Akhavan Comes of Age." *Washington Post*, 15 January. https://www.washington post.com/goingoutguide/movies/appropriate-behavior-movie-review

desiree-akhavan-comes-of-age/2015/01/14/2fba0a90-9825-11e4-927a-4fa2638cd1b0_story.html.
Moddelmog, Debra A. 2009. "Can *Romantic Comedy* Be Gay? Hollywood Romance, Citizenship, and Same-Sex Marriage Panic." *Journal of Popular Film and Television* 36, no. 4: 162–73.
Monaghan, Whitney. 2016. *Queer Girls, Temporality, and Screen Media: Not "Just a Phase."* Basingstoke: Palgrave Macmillan.
Naficy, Hamid. 2001. *An Accented Cinema: Exilic and Diasporic Filmmaking.* Princeton: Princeton University Press.
Nagle, Angela. 2017. *Kill All Normies: Online Culture Wars from 4Chan and Tumblr to Trump and the Alt-Right.* Winchester, UK: Zero.
Ng, Eve. 2013. "A 'Post-Gay' Era? Media Gaystreaming, Homonormativity, and the Politics of LGBT Integration." *Communication, Culture and Critique* 6, no. 2: 258–83.
Nicholson, Amy. 2014. "Who Killed the Romantic Comedy?" *LA Weekly*, 27 February. http://www.laweekly.com/news/who-killed-the-romantic-comedy-4464884.
Northrup, Andrew. 2018. "Revitalizing the Teen Movie: An Interview with Desiree Akhavan." *Cineaste* 43, no. 4 (Fall): 22–5.
Onion. 1999. "Romantic-Comedy Behavior Gets Real-Life Man Arrested." *The Onion*, 7 April. https://local.theonion.com/romantic-comedy-behavior-gets-real-life-man-arrested-1819565117.
Out.com. 2012. "Out100 2012: Ingrid Jungermann & Desiree Akhavan." *Out*, 15 November. https://www.out.com/out-exclusives/out100-2012/2012/11/15/out100-ingrid-jungermann-desiree-akhavan.
Perkins, Claire. 2016. "My Effortless Brilliance: Women's Mumblecore." In *Indie Reframed: Women's Filmmaking and Contemporary American Independent Cinema*, edited by Linda Badley, Claire Perkins, and Michele Schreiber, 138–53. Edinburgh: Edinburgh University Press.
Perkins, Claire, and Constantine Verevis. 2012. "Introduction: Three Times." In *Film Trilogies: New Critical Approaches*, edited by Claire Perkins and Constantine Verevis, 1–31. Basingstoke, UK: Palgrave Macmillan.

Press, Joy. 2018. "Desiree Akhavan Has a Bisexual Awakening on New Hulu Series." *Vanity Fair*, 13 November. https://www.vanityfair.com/hollywood/2018/11/desiree-akhavan-interview-on-new-hulu-show-the-bisexual.

Rich, B. Ruby. 1992. "A Queer Sensation." *Village Voice*, 24 March: 41–4.

— 2013. *New Queer Cinema: The Director's Cut*. Durham: Duke University Press.

Richards, Stuart James. 2017. *The Queer Film Festival: Popcorn and Politics*. New York: Palgrave Macmillan.

Rooney, David. 2014. "Appropriate Behavior: Sundance Review." *Hollywood Reporter*, 18 January. https://www.hollywoodreporter.com/review/appropriate-behavior-sundance-review-672264.

San Filippo, Maria. 2019. "Breaking Upwards: The Creative Uncoupling of Desiree Akhavan and Ingrid Jungermann." In *Independent Women: From Film to Television*, special issue of *Feminist Media Studies* 19, no. 7: 991–1008.

— 2020a. *Provocauteurs and Provocations: Screening Sex in 21st Century Media*. Bloomington: Indiana University Press.

— 2020b. "Serial Offender: *The Bisexual* (2018)." *Journal of Bisexuality* 20, no. 3: 233–43.

— Forthcoming. "Living in the Gray Area: Bisexual Signification in Desiree Akhavan's *The Bisexual*." In *Television Studies in Queer Times*, edited by Hollis Griffin. New York: Routledge.

SBS. 2019. "In *The Bisexual*, Desiree Akhavan Is Here to Explore the Last Taboo." *SBS*, 10 December. https://www.sbs.com.au/guide/article/2019/12/10/bisexual-desiree-akhavan-here-explore-last-taboo.

Sconce, Jeffrey. 2002. "Irony, Nihilism, and the New American 'Smart' Film." *Screen* 43, no. 4 (Winter): 349–69.

Schoonover, Karl. 2012. "Wastrels of Time: Slow Cinema's Laboring Body, the Political Spectator, and the Queer." *Journal of Cinema and Media* 53, no. 1: 65–78.

Scott, A.O. 2018. "My Woody Allen Problem." *New York Times*, 31 January. https://www.nytimes.com/2018/01/31/movies/woody-allen.html.
Secher, Benjamin. 2005. "Catherine Breillat: 'All True Artists Are Hated.'" *Telegraph* [London], 8 April. https://www.telegraph.co.uk/culture/film/starsandstories/3672302/Catherine-BreillatAll-true-artists-are-hated.html.
Sedgwick, Eve Kosofsky. 2008 [1990]. *Epistemology of the Closet*. Berkeley: University of California Press.
Sen, Sharmila. 2018. *Not Quite White: Losing and Finding Race in America*. New York: Penguin.
Setoodeh, Ramin. 2014. "Sundance: Why Desiree Akhavan Could be the Next Lena Dunham." *Variety*, 18 January. https://variety.com/2014/film/marketsfestivals/.
Shihani, Nishant. 2011. *Queer Retrosexualities: The Politics of Reparative Return*. Bethlehem: Lehigh University Press.
Stanford, Eleanor. 2018. "In *The Bisexual*, Desiree Akhavan Grapples with All Kinds of Sexuality." *New York Times*, 13 November. https://www.nytimes.com/2018/11/13/arts/television/the-bisexual-desiree-akhavan-hulu.html.
Stevens, Kyle. 2015. "The Graduate and the Subversion of Silence." In *Mike Nichols: Sex, Language, and the Reinvention of Psychological Realism*. Oxford: Oxford University Press.
Stockton, Kathryn Bond. 2009. *The Queer Child, or Growing Sideways in the Twentieth Century*. Durham: Duke University Press.
Stoller, Matt. 2019. "The Slow Death of Hollywood." *Big* [Newsletter], 9 July. https://mattstoller.substack.com/p/the-slow-death-of-hollywood.
Symons, Alex. 2013. "The Problem of 'High Culture' Comedy: How *Annie Hall* (1977) Complicated Woody Allen's Reputation." *Journal of Popular Film and Television* 41, no. 3 (July): 118–27.
Tatevosian, Mare. 2014. "You're My Only Hope: A Love Letter to Desiree Akhavan." Girls on Tops [Blog], 14 February. https://www.girlsontopstees.

com/read-me/2020/2/14/youre-my-only-hope-a-love-letter-to-desiree-akhavan.

Ward, Cameron. 2015. "Desiree Akhavan Talks *Appropriate Behavior*, *Girls* and Directing Yourself." *One Room with a View*, 8 March. https://oneroomwithaview.com/2015/03/08/desiree-akhavan-talks-appropriate-behaviour-girls-and-directing-yourself/.

White, Patricia. 2015. *Women's Cinema, World Cinema: Projecting Contemporary Feminisms* Durham: Duke University Press.

Wickham, Celia. 2015. "Interview with Desiree Akhavan," *Berlin Film Journal*, May 2015. http://berlinfilmjournal.com/2015/05/interview-with-desiree-akhavan/.

Mediography

Film

Akhavan, Desiree, dir. 2013. *Appropriate Behavior*. Kino Lorber, 2013. DVD.
– dir. 2018. *The Miseducation of Cameron Post*. FilmRise, 2018. DVD.
Allen, Woody, dir. 1977. *Annie Hall*. MGM Home Entertainment, 2002. DVD.
– dir. 1979. *Manhattan*. 20th Century Fox Home Entertainment, 2007. DVD.
Babbit, Jamie, dir. 1999. *But I'm a Cheerleader*. A Plus Entertainment, 2000. DVD.
Baumbach, Noah, dir. 2005. *The Squid and the Whale*. Criterion Collection, 2016. DVD.
– dir. 2007. *Margot at the Wedding*. Paramount Home Entertainment, 2008. DVD.
Breillat, Catherine, dir. 2001. *À ma soeur (Fat Girl)*. Criterion Collection, 2004. DVD.
Cholodenko, Lisa, dir. 1998. *High Art*. Universal Studios Home Video, 2004. DVD.
– dir. 2010. *The Kids Are All Right*. Universal Pictures Home Entertainment, 2010. DVD.

Heise, William, dir. 1896. *The Kiss* (May Irwin Kiss). Library of Congress (YouTube), 2009. https://www.youtube.com/watch?v=Q69o-IexNB4.
Hitchcock, Alfred, dir. 1963. *The Birds*. Universal Pictures Home Entertainment, 2020. DVD.
Jungermann, Ingrid, dir. 2016. *Women Who Kill*. FilmRise, 2017. Digital.
Kechiche, Abdellatif, dir. 2013. *La vie d'Adèle (Blue Is the Warmest Color)*. Criterion Collection, 2014. DVD.
Keshavarz, Maryan, dir. 2011. *Circumstance*. Peccadillo Pictures, 2012. DVD.
Nichols, Mike, dir. 1967. *The Graduate*. MGM Home Entertainment, 1999. DVD.
Ophüls, Marcel, dir. 1969. *Le chagrin et la pitié (The Sorrow and the Pity)*. Oscilloscope, 2011. DVD.
Troche, Rose, dir. 1994. *Go Fish*. The Samuel Goldwyn Company, n.d. DVD.
Welles, Orson, dir. 1941. *Citizen Kane*. Warner Home Video, 2016. DVD.

Television and Web Series

Akhavan, Desiree, and Ingrid Jungermann. 2010–12. *The Slope*. USA: Vimeo.
Akhavan, Desiree, and Rowan Riley. 2018. *The Bisexual*. UK/US: Channel 4 Television/Hulu.
Bergman, Ingmar, dir. 1973. *Scenes from a Marriage*. Criterion Collection, 1973. DVD.
Blichfeld, Katja, and Ben Sinclair. 2012–15, 2016–20. *High Maintenance*. USA: Vimeo, Home Box Office.
Chaiken, Ilene. 2004–09. *The L Word*. USA: Showtime Networks.
– 2010–12. *The Real L Word*. USA: Showtime Networks.
Dunham, Lena. 2012–17. *Girls*. USA: Home Box Office.
Glazer, Ilana, and Abbi Jacobson. 2010–11, 2014–19. *Broad City*. USA: YouTube, Comedy Central.
Jungermann, Ingrid. 2013–14. *F to 7th*. USA: www.fto7th.com.
Rae, Issa. 2011, 2016–21. *Misadventures of Awkward Black Girl (Insecure)*. USA: YouTube; Home Box Office.
Star, Darren. 1998–2004. *Sex and the City*. USA: Home Box Office.

Music

"Oh Sombra! [John Peel Session]." 2004. On *Singles, B-Sides & Live*. Lyrics by Juan Boscán Almogávar. Performed by Electrelane. Published by Chrysalis Music Ltd.

"To the East." 2007. On *No Shouts, No Calls*. Written by Mia Clarke, Emma Gaze, Rosamund Murray and Verity Susman. Performed by Electrelane. BMG Music. Published by Chrysalis Music Ltd.

Index

Page numbers in italics indicate references to illustrations.

400 Blows, The (1959), 121

À ma soeur (2001). See *Fat Girl*
Academy Awards, 9, 20, 44, 47, 93
Academy of Motion Picture Arts and Sciences, 24
Adsit, Scott, xiv, *12*
AfterEllen, 29
Ahmadinejad, Mahmoud, 64
Airplane! (1981), 44
Akhavan, Desiree: alter egos of, 11–12, 28–9, 34–6, 38, 48, 75–6, 78, 84, 95, 98, 107; as bisexual, 6–7, 14–15, 28–9, 37–8, 57, 70, 81–5, 87, 92, 94, 96–9, 111, 118–19, 122–3, 125–6; body image of, 41–2, 85, 129, 138n7; and Lena Dunham, 9, 12–13, *13*, 37–8, *38*, 41, 85; early life of, 15, 41–2, 57, 83, 85, 94, 96, 121–2, 129, 137n2, 139n8; experience of coming out, 94, 96; film(maker) influences on, 4, 17, 21–2, 23, 93, 106, 116–18; as in-betweener, 14–15, 28, 70–1, 82, 84, 98–9; as Iranian American, 7, 14–15, 37–8, 64, 70, 81–94, 117, 119, 125, 128, 137n2; perception of *Annie Hall*, 4, 43, 45–6, 116–18; perception of *Appropriate Behavior*, 4–5, 79, 117, 120; perception of web series, 27; perception of (romantic) comedy, 47, 121–2, 126; performing nude, 38–9; persona of, 11, 14, 85; perspective on feminism, 21; perspective on Hollywood's gender politics, 46, 110, 132; perspective on the male gaze, 24; taste in media, 17, 19, 23, 29, 81; use of language, 6, 28, 54, 100, 106, 122–3
All Over Me (1997), 17
Allen, Woody, 36, 43, 45–8, *51*, 54, 76, 79, 106, 115–17, 138n1
Almogávar, Juan Boscán, 52, 135
Amirpour, Ana Lily, 93
Annie Hall (1977), 4, 34, 36, 43–4, *44*, 45–51, *51*, 52–8, *58*, 59–79, 106, 113, 116–18, 121, 137n4, 138nn1–2
anti-Semitism, 62–3, 67
Appropriate Behavior (2014): acclaim for, 8–9; as autobiographical, 17, 28, 34, 48, 52, 78, 81, 90, 107–8; bisexuality in, 3, 13–15, 48–9, 70, 73, 82, 97–9, 99–102, 104–5, 111, 113, 125–6; cast and crew of, xiii–xiv, 11, 17–18, *18*,

120; citation in, 17–18, *18*, 29–30, 73, 78, *80*, 139n5; as coming-out film, 20, 62, 65, 70–4, 86, 92, 104–5, 107–9, 119, 127; connection to Mumblecore, 23; crossover appeal of, 8–9, 14–16, 20, 28, 98–9; development of, 24, 34, 45, 85, 117–18; distribution of, 9, 13, 15; as feminist film, 21, 46, 48, 74, 93; financing of, 7, 11; as first feature, 4, 7–10, 15, 17, 42, 121; as independent film, 5, 7–9, 12; as in-betweener film, 15, 23, 70–1, 98–9; as Iranian American film, 7, 9, 11, 13–15, 48, 70, 82–94, 125; irony in, 4, 12, 17, 19–20, 72, 78, 117; as love story, 3, 118–19, 126; marketing of, 11–13, *13*, 14, 28, 40, 104, 131; narrative structure of, 7, 52, 70–1, 76; as queer film (classic), 3–9, 14, 24, 113, 122; (post)feminist discourse in, 39, 57; production of, 11–12, *12*, 36, 115–16; as (radical) romantic comedy, 3–4, 48–50, 70–4, 106, 121; reception of, 7–9, 14–15, 24–5, 47, 71, 97, 110, 130; relation to *Annie Hall*, 4, 34, 43, 45–51, *51*, 53–8, *58*, 59–79, 106, 116, 137n4; synopsis of, xi–xiv; as trilogy, 4–5; as smart film, 33; as woman-made film, 3, 7, 11, 14, 24
Arabian Nights (1974), 4
Argo (2012), 129
Asghar, Fatimah, 26

Babeland, 59
Bailey, Sam, 26
Barnes, Beanie, 10
Baumbach, Noah, 33, 37, 106, 116
Beaches (1988), 101
Beauvoir, Simone de, 56
Becker, Ernest, 56
Benson, Chloe, 97

Bergman, Ingmar, 54, *80*, 106
Bigelow, Kathryn, 47
Birds, The (1963), 78
Birds of Prey (2020), 140n1
bisexual: erasure, 36, 95–6, 105, 138n6; identity, 15, 82–3, 95–6, 105; invisibility, 85, 95, 99–100; woman (of colour), 3, 6–7, 11–13, 15, 28–9, 48, 98, 112
Bisexual, The (2018), 4, 11, 36–7, 41–2, 82–3, 94, 111–12, 114, 119, 123, 125, 127–8, 131
bisexuality: cultural conceptions of, 96–8, 101–2, 105; representation of, 3, 95–9, 102–4, 111–13, 123–4; stereotypes of, 3, 9, 11, 84, 102–4, 123; as taboo, 94, 111–12. *See also* bisexual
Black Widow (2021), 140n1
Blazing Saddles (1974), 44
Blichfeld, Katja, 26
Blue Is the Warmest Color (2013), 24
Bluestockings, 59, 122
Bob & Carol & Ted & Alice (1969), 44
Bordieu, Pierre, 79
Bound (1996), 99
Boys in the Sand (1971), 4
Bradbury-Rance, Clara, 139n5
Breillat, Catherine, 21–2, *22*, 79
Brickman, Marshall, 65, 138n1
Bridesmaids (2011), 48
Broad City (2014–19), 26, 34
Brooklyn, NY, xi–xiii, 7, 11–13, 17, 25, 49–50, 52, 59, 64, 67–8, *68*, 69, 92, 100, 131. *See also* New York City
Brown Girls (2017)
Buskfilms, 20
But I'm a Cheerleader (1999), 17, 131, *133*
Butler, Judith, 70

Call Me by Your Name (2017), 97
cancel culture, 34
canon, film, 3–5. *See also* queer film: canon
Caro, Niki, 140n1
Chana, Saskia, 36, 127
Chasing Amy (1997), 99
Chávez, Linda Yvette, 26
Cholodenko, Lisa, 16–18, *18*, 20, 22, 79
Christian, Aymar Jean, 26
Circumstance (2011), 93–5
Citizen Kane (1941), 101–2
chrononormativity, 71
Clarkson, Patricia, 17
Coel, Michaela, 34
comedy: anti-intellectual, 69, 79; history of American, 44–5; inappropriate, 9, 34, 49, 54, 59, 62, 100, 124–5; indie, 7; ironic, 19–20, 24, 27, 29–30, 32–3, 100, 125; Jewish, 48, 50, 62–3, *63*, 79; politically incorrect, 12, 19, 29, 32, 49–50, 52, 125; scatological, 4, 79, 112, 121; uncoupling, 44, 48, 54, 73–4, 109, 121, 138n2. *See also* romantic comedy
Comedy Central, 26
coming-out film. *See* queer film: coming-out stories in
COVID-19 pandemic, 11, 112–13, 140n1
Crazy Rich Asians (2018), 48
crossover film. *See* queer film: crossover
Cumming, Alan, 140n4

Danforth, Emily, 110
Day, Doris, 45
D.E.B.S. (2004), 19
DeFranco, Cody, xiv, 121
Denial of Death, The (1973), 56, *58*
dildo, xi, 59, 67, 69, 76–7, *77*, 109

distribution: digital, 20, 27, 137n1; indie, 7–8, 14–15, 27; niche, 26; theatrical, 8–9. *See also* streaming media
Drugstore Cowboy (1989), 9
Duggan, Lisa, 15–16
Dunham, Lena, 9, 12–13, *13*, 37–8, *38*, 41, 45, 83, 85
Duong, Anh, xiv, 17–18, *18*, 83
Duplass, Mark, 10–11, 23
Duplass brothers (Mark and Jay), 23

Electrelane, 52, *55*, 73, 92, 139n7
Enchanted (2007), 44
Ephron, Nora, 47
Eternals (2021), 140n1

F to 7th (2013–14), 34
Farahani, Golshifteh, 93
Farhadi, Asghar, 93
fart jokes. *See* comedy: scatological
Fassbinder, Rainer Werner, 17
Fat Girl (2001), 22, 115, 117
Feiffer, Halley, xiv, 36, 121, 139n6
Feinberg, Leslie, 56
Female Trouble (1974), 4
feminist film: homage to, 21–2, 22; legacy of, 93. *See also* women filmmakers
Fennell, Emerald, 34
Fey, Tina, 129
film festivals, 8–9, 14; LGBTQ+, 7–8, 137n1. *See also* South by Southwest Film Festival; Sundance Film Festival
Fleabag (2016–19), 34
Freeman, Elizabeth, 71, 90
Fresh Air, 4, 6, 20, 28, 36, 41, 49, 64, 82, 87
Frugiuele, Cecilia, ix, xiii, 24, 36, 85, 101, 110–11, 116, 118, 128, 130, 132

gay cinema. *See* queer film
gay conversion therapy, 110, 131, 138n7
gay marriage. *See* marriage equality
gaze: female, 22, 115; male, 24, 115; queer, 115–16
gender transitioning, 54, 59
Gentefied (2017; 2020–21), 26
Gershon, Gina, 99
Gerwig, Greta, 22–3
Girl Walks Home Alone at Night, A (2014), 93
Girlfriends (1978), 138n2
Girls (2012–17), 37–8, *38*, 94
Girls on Tops, 24–5, *25*, 87
Girls Trip (2017), 48
GLAAD, 9, 15
Glazer, Ilana, 26
Glee (2009–15), 26
Go Fish (1996), 17, 99, 109, 137n4
Graduate, The (1967), 45, 73, 75
Grand Illusion (1937), 61
Gravitas Ventures, xiv, 9
Graziano, Annalisa, xiv, 140n5
Greene Bricmont, Wendy, 45
Gross, Terry, 4

Hacks (2021–), 134
Halberstam, Jack, 16, 30–1, 36, 138n6
Halperin, David M., 15, 20
Hannah Takes the Stairs (2007), 23
Harold and Maude (1971), 44
Harrison, Rebecca, 5
Happiness (1998), 33
Heche, Anne, 97, 140n4
Hedwig and the Angry Inch (2001), 19
Henderson, Rebecca, xiv, 121
Herbie Fully Loaded (2005), 140n1

heteronormativity, 4, 15–16, 20, 30, 36, 44, 70, 90, 100
High Art (1997), 16–18, *18*, 137n3
High Maintenance (2012–20), 26, 34
hipster culture, 7, 17, 50, 52, 59, 67
Holm, Liz, 115
Holofcener, Nicole, 33
homonormativity, 15–16, 20, 30, 36, 70, 72, 109
Hudson, Rock, 45
Hulu, 111
Husbands and Wives (1992), 115

I Love You Phillip Morris (2009), 19
I May Destroy You (2020), 34
IFC (Independent Film Channel), 26
in-betweener, 14–15, 70–1, 82, 98–9
independent cinema: creative autonomy in, 22; financing of, 7–9; history of, 17, 22–3; market for, 8–16, 25, 27, 111, 132. *See also* distribution: indie; Mumblecore
Independent Spirit Awards, 9, 15
IndieWire, 24
Insecure (2016–21), 26, 34
intersectionality, 97, 112, 127–8, 139n1
Iran, 63–4, 86, 92–4, 128–9, 137n2
Iranian: Americans, 86–8; culture, 92, 108, 125; cultural expectations of, 11, 13, 85–9, 128; diaspora, 85–7, 93, 125; discourse in *Appropriate Behavior*, 86, 92–4, 125–6; political regime of, 63–4, 86; stereotypical representation of, 7, 84, 86, 93. *See also* Nowruz
irony. *See* comedy: ironic
Islamophobia, 84, 93
It Gets Better, 30–1, *31*

Jacobson, Abbi, 26, 140n4
Jeffers McDonald, Tamar, 44
Jenkins, Barry, 20–1
Jenkins, Patty, 140n1
Jules et Jim (1963), 116
Jungermann, Ingrid, 17, 25, 27–31, 33–6, 45, 100, 117–18, 124

Keaton, Diane, 36, 48–9
Keshavarz, Maryam, 93
Kicking and Screaming (1995), 33
Kickstarter, 26, 50
Kids Are All Right, The (2010), 16, 20, 24, 99
Kino Lorber, xiv, 12
Kirschner, Marcus, 115, 124
Kiss, The (1896), 78, *80*
Knife in the Water (1962), 116

L Word, The (2004–09), 26, 29–31
LA. *See* Los Angeles
Lady Bird (2017), 23
Le Tigre, 139n7
lesbian cinema, 4, 8n1, 16–*18*, 19–20, 24
lesbians, lesbianism: audience, 24, 29; representation of, 16–17, 24, 98–9, 122; terminology, 6, 19, 28–9, 49–50, 54, 98
LGBTQ+ cinema. *See* queer film
LGBTQ+ identity, 3; politics, 15–16, 32, 56, 59, 65, 92. *See also* queer
LGBTQ+ film festivals. *See* film festivals: LGBTQ+
Little Fires Everywhere (2020), 23
LOGO, 26
Los Angeles, 61, 67, 70
Lost Highway (1997), 9
Love, Heather K., 61

Lubitsch, Ernst, 45

Magic Mike (2012), 48
Makhmalbaf, Hana, 93
Makhmalbaf, Marzieh, 93
Makhmalbaf, Samira, 93
Manhattan (1979), 116, 138n1
Manhattan Murder Mystery (1993), 138n1
Marañón, Miren, xiii, 116
Margot at the Wedding (2007), 115
marriage equality, 15, 17. *See also Obergefell v. Hodges*
Marriage Story (2019), 106
Martel, Lucrecia, 47
Mayer, So, 138n4
McDermott, Catherine, 40, 57, 92
McLuhan, Marshall, 77
#MeToo, 5, 24, 41, 54
Meyers, Nancy, 47, 140n1
Millennials, 9, 29, 50, 67
Misadventures of Awkward Black Girl (2011–13), 26, 34
Miseducation of Cameron Post, The, 41, 110–11, 115, 131–3, *133*, 138n7, 139n1
Mitchell, John Cameron, 19
Moddelmog, Debra A., 16
Modern Family (2009–20), 26
Monáe, Janelle, 140n4
Moonlight (2016), 20–1
Monaghan, Whitney, 71
Moore, Julianne, 99
Moretz, Chloë Grace, 110, 131
Mulan (2020), 140n1
Mullins, Aimee, xiv, 83, *84*, 120, 139n2
Mumblecore, 23, 79

Naficy, Hamid, 92
Nair, Mira, 140n1
neoliberalism, 16
Neshat, Shirin, 93, 137n4
Netflix. *See* streaming media
New Queer Cinema, 17–18, *18*, 20
New York City, 11, 15, 17, 64–8, *68*, 72. *See also* Brooklyn, NY
New York University, 11, 23, 25, 27–8, 79, 85, 106, 121, 137n2
Nichols, Mike, 45
Nicholson, Amy, 47
Nights and Weekends (2008), 23
nonlinear narrative, 7, 52, 70–1, 76, 94–5, 116. *See also* queer: temporality
Nose Job (2010), 11, 85, 138n7
Nowruz, xi, xii, 86–8, 90, 92, 107–8, 126. *See also* Iranian: Americans
NYU. *See* New York University

Obergefell v. Hodges, 32, 64, 137n5
Obvious Child (2014), 115
Old Guard, The (2020), 140n1
Ophüls, Marcel, 62
Orange Is the New Black (2013–19), 26
Oscars. *See* Academy Awards

Panahi, Jafar, 93
Parent Trap, The (1998), 140n1
Pariah (2011), 20–1
Park Slope Coop, xi, 57, *63*, 70
Parkville Pictures, ix, xiii
Party Girl (1995), 17
Patreon, 26
PC (politically correct) culture, 11–12, 19, 29, 32, 34. *See also* comedy: political incorrect
Peake, Maxine, 111

Peccadillo Pictures, xiv, 9
Perkins, Claire, 14, 23, 71
Persepolis (2007), 93
Persia. *See* Iran
Philadelphia (1992), 20
Pillow Talk (1959), 45
Polanski, Roman, 116
pornography, 4, 24, 99
Pretty Woman (1990), 44
Pride, xii, 76, 102, 106
Prince-Bythewood, Gina, 140n1
Private Benjamin (1980), 138n2
Promising Young Woman (2020), 34
Puccini for Beginners (2006), 97

Queen of Katwe (2016), 140n1
queer: culture, 14, 17, 19–20, 57, 64; history, 35, 62; ideology, 15–16, 29, 70, 90; as mode of critique, 3–5, 15, 20, 30–1, 36; people of colour, 112, 139n1; queer-feminist praxis, 35–7; reappropriation, 5, 19–20, 28; representation, 26–7, 29, 127–8; temporality, 4, 70–1, 90, 95; terminology, 6, 14, 19–20, 28, 96, 98; victimhood, 64. *See also* LGBTQ+ identity
queer film: audiences, 9, 16, 26, 29, 32, 98–9, 122; canon, 3–5; classics, 3–5; comedy, 19–20, 32; coming-out stories in, 4, 20, 70–4, 107, 110, 124; creators, 19, 26; crossover, 8–9, 14–16, 24, 26, 98–9; distribution, 9; failure, 35–6, 90; homage, 17–18, *18*, 49; market for, 4, 13–16, 20; universalism of, 3, 19–20. *See also* New Queer Cinema
QueerFrame, 20

Rae, Issa, 26
Rannells, Andrew, 94

Real L Word, The (2010–12), 29
Rees, Dee, 20–1
Renoir, Jean, 61
reproductive futurism, 71, 90
Rich, B. Ruby, 17, 20
Rich and Famous (1981), 44n2
Robespierre, Gillian, 137n3
Robinson, Angela, 19, 140n1
romantic comedy, bourgeois ideology of, 33, 44–5; cultural perceptions of, 4; gay and lesbian, 16–17, 19, 48–50, 131; marketplace for, 44–5, 47–8; queering of, 48–51, *51*, 70–4, 109; straightness of, 16, 72; radical, 44–5, 73; tropes of 16, 49, 50–1, *51*, 59, 74, 109, 126, 131, 138n3; whiteness of, 16, 48, 126; women-created, 47
Rosenblum, Ralph, 45
Russell, David O., 33

Sachs, Ira, xiii, 27–8
Samson, JD, 139n7
Satrapi, Marjane, 93
Savage, Dan, 30
Scenes from a Marriage (1974), 106, 117
Sconce, Jeffrey, 33
Scorpio Rising (1963), 4
Scott, A.O., 46
Second Sex, The (1949), 56–7, 60
Sedgwick, Eve Kosofsky, 70
Seventh Seal, The (1957), 79
Sex and the City (1998–2004), 29, 57
sex scenes, 21, 24, 40–1, 52
Shampoo (1975), 138n2
Shaw, Sara, xiii, 116, 130, 139n7
Sheedy, Ally, 17
Shelton, Lynn, 22–3
Shihani, Nishant, 62

Shining, The (1980), 79
Shortland, Cate, 140n1
Showalter, Michael, 28
Simon, Paul, 61
Simon and Garfunkel, 73
Sleeper (1973), 44n1
Slope, The (2010–12), 4, 7, 11, 14, 17, 20, 26–31, *31*, 32–5, 52, 54, 70, 95, 98, 100, 117, 124–5
slurs. *See* queer: terminology
smart film, 33
Smith College, 57, 96, 107–8, *108*, 140n3
Solondz, Todd, 33
Sorrow and the Pity, The (1969), 62, 65–6, 66
South by Southwest Film Festival, 10–11, 23
Spanking the Monkey (1994), 33
split screen, 45
Squid and the Whale, The (2005), 139n6
Star Wars (1977), 44
Star Wars: Rogue Squadron (2023), 140n1
Stockton, Kathryn Bond, 4
Stone Butch Blues (1993), xi, 56–8, *58*, 60, 65–6, 66, 92, 122
Stranger than Paradise (1984), 121
strap-on. *See* dildo
streaming media, 7–10, 20, 27, 129
Sundance Film Festival, xiv, 7–9, 14–15, 23, 28, 47, 110–11, 130
Sunday Bloody Sunday (1971), 97
Swanberg, Joe, 23

Teague, Chris, xiii, 115–16, 137n3
television: adapted web series in, 34; contemporary, 10–11; indie, 26–7; legacy, 27, 34; queer content in, 20, 26–7, 29–30, 33, 111
Tequila, Tila, 97, 140n4
Thomas, Jonathan Taylor, 7

threesome, 12, 40, 56, 72, 102–3, 120, 131, 138n3
Tilly, Jennifer, 99
Trainwreck (2015), 48
Trash (1970), 4
Turner, Guinevere, 137n4
Twardziak, Allison, xiii, 11, 121
Twitter, 21–2, 22, 24

Under the Shadow (2016), 129
Unmarried Woman, An (1978), 44n2

Vimeo, 26, 28
VOD (video on demand). *See* distribution: digital

Walking and Talking (1997), 1997
Waller-Bridge, Phoebe, 34

We Go Way Back (2006), 22–3
web series, 4, 21, 25–35. See also *The Slope* (2010–12)
Weight of Water, The (2000), 47–8
White, Patricia, 93
Wiggs, Josephine, xiii, 73n7
women media creators, 3, 8, 16–17, 21–2, 22, 23–5, 33, 37, 46–8, 93, 106, 132, 140n1. *See also* feminist film
Women Who Kill (2016), 28, 36
Wood, Evan Rachel, 140n4

Yaghmaei, Kourosh, 108
Yan, Cathy, 140n1
You Can Count on Me (2000), 72n6
YouTube, 26

Zhao, Chloé, 140n1